Laurence W. M. (Laurence William Maxwell Lockhart

Fair to see

Vol. I

Laurence W. M. (Laurence William Maxwell Lockhart

Fair to see
Vol. I

ISBN/EAN: 9783337051594

Printed in Europe, USA, Canada, Australia, Japan

Cover: Foto ©ninafisch / pixelio.de

More available books at **www.hansebooks.com**

FAIR TO SEE

A NOVEL

BY

LAURENCE W. M. LOCKHART

AUTHOR OF 'DOUBLES AND QUITS'

IN THREE VOLUMES

VOL. I.

WILLIAM BLACKWOOD AND SONS
EDINBURGH AND LONDON
MDCCCLXXI

The Right of Translation is reserved

FAIR TO SEE.

CHAPTER I.

The shooting season of the year 186-, —the great and glorious "Twelfth,"—was drawing near, and the prospects and the hopes therewith connected were one wet Sunday afternoon the subject of deep discussion in the mess-room of the —th, then quartered in the New Barracks at Gosport. The regiment had very lately returned from a tour of foreign service; and this circumstance entitled the officers to two months' extra leave of absence, as soon and in such proportions as they could be spared from "duty." About half of their number, made up of those who did not specially affect sport, and of those whose juniority deprived them of a voice in the matter, were already availing themselves of this privilege; and thus the approaching months of August and September were left open to those who remained behind — gentlemen for whom the crow of the "muir-cock" and the whirr of the partridge were that very soul of music for which they had been yearning all the last four years in a tropical station.

The company, therefore, lounging in the mess-room after church-parade and luncheon on the Sunday in question, being mostly of one persuasion as to sport—with one faith, one hope, and, for the present at least, one idea—formed a harmonious and happy assemblage, and the common idea was very thoroughly ventilated. The special qualities of the old "muzzler," the various modifications of the "pin" breech-loader and the "central-fire," the rival merits of Henry, and Dickson, and Purdey & Dougall, were gone into at full length; pointers and setters, retrievers and terriers—dogs of all degrees—had their due share of attention; nor, in the exhaustive treatment of the subject, was a place denied to the minor equipments of the "shikari," which were all laid on the *tapis*, and sat upon with the solemnity befitting subjects of such grave importance.

Sportsmen—or, as we should perhaps rather say, men talking about sport — are apt to repeat themselves; and undoubtedly this tendency to iteration is one of the deadliest nuisances to which flesh, in club and smoking room, is heir. Who does not tremble when the hunting Munchausen gets into his saddle? when the nautical proser clears out of harbour? when the shooting Bore plants his foot upon his native heath, and opens fire with his monotonous barrels?

But here, all being of the same mind, none were dissatisfied; and though every one who had an idea or an opinion repeated it emphatically not less than seventeen or eighteen times, the hearing vouchsafed to each successive utterance was perfectly patient and respectful. Why not? Here all interests were respected, here perfect reciprocity was established; and under such circumstances, this conversational method has the very tangible advantage of killing a wet afternoon with a minimum tear and wear of cerebral tissue, of which we can never be too saving. By degrees the conversation passed to the plans and prospects of individuals for the next two months.

"What lucky fellows are going north for the 'Twelfth'?" asked one of the party.

"I am," and "I am," and "I am," rose from several voices.

"AND I AM!" cried Fuskisson, a little white ensign, speaking in large capitals with a voice like a Jew's harp.

"And I am NOT!" shouted M'Niven, the adjutant—a large, loud, red, portentous-looking Scot, whose nationality, combined with certain peculiarities of diction, had procured for him the sobriquet of "Ossian."

"But I AM," persisted Fuskisson, as if in that fact M'Niven ought to find ample compensation. "Old Gosset, my father's partner, has again come to the front; and this will be my second innings at Braxy. Luck for me, isn't it? Braxy *is* something like a billet. You can bag your five-and-twenty brace there any day, don't you know? besides hooking your salmon in Kelt water in the morning, don't you see? and then the feeding and the liquor, mind you! Pass that bottle of sherry, some one, that I may drink old Gosset's health."

"Pearls cast unto the swine!" thundered M'Niven. "Pearls cast utterly to a very foul sort of swine, pale-faced descendant of the Fuski! It has now come to this, that huckstering aldermen, — bloated, gouty-hooved, asthmatic, turtle-eating aldermen,—with their puny brood of aldermanikins like you, desecrate the heather, demoralise the game, and suck up all the ozone from Scotia's violated breezes; while I, Niven, sad son of Niven and of the mountain, pine grouseless in this southern cell."

"Are you really going to pine all the leave-season in your southern cell, Ossian?" asked Fuskisson, who took the adjutant's magniloquent personalities with perfect composure.

"'My poverty, but not my will, consents.'"

"Neither my poverty nor my will consents," said Bertrand Cameron, a handsome, smart-looking subaltern; "but, all the same, it seems as if I were doomed to share Ossian's cell with him. Here am I with the frugal savings of two years, saved for the very purpose of getting some shooting in Scotland when we came home; here am I, author of seven advertisements on the subject, still unprovided with a moor; that is, Pigott and I—for, of course, I could not go in for the whole thing by myself; so as Pigott is in the same boat with me, he will make a third for the cell, if something doesn't turn up soon."

"Have you looked in to-day's 'Field'?" asked one of the party.

"No, I haven't. Has it come?"

"Yes; and I heard some of the fellows at breakfast reading and laughing over an advertisement of a Scotch shooting in it."

"Oh! a 'Tommiebeg,' I suppose."

"I don't know: you'd better have a look at it."

"I wonder where it is."

"Dent took it to his room after breakfast," said Fuskisson. "I saw him going away with it."

"Well, as he's your captain, you're responsible for him; go and bring it, and tell him he's fined."

"I daren't go near him just now; he's awfully savage at me. Fancy his cheek! he ordered me to come and load cartridges for him till luncheon; and when I told him it was against my principles to labour on Sunday, he said, 'All right; it's against my principles to pay the company for the next fortnight, so you must do it, my boy.' And when I said, 'Hang it, that's fagging,' he said, ' Mr Fuskisson, you mustn't use insubordinate language on the Sabbath-day in your captain's quarters; leave them, sir, and pay the men for the next three weeks; another such expression and I'll make it a month, and cut you out of Braxy altogether.' The beast! why did you post me to his company, Ossian ?"

"Dent is wise!" thundered M'Niven — "Dent is a philosopher; Dent, by the Mass, is Scriptural! he spares not the rod, lest he spoil this Cockney bantling."

"I'll send a mess-waiter for it, then," said Cameron; and in due time the paper was brought and examined by one of the party.

"Here it is," he cried, with a laugh, after scanning the columns for a minute or two. "Here it is—and the very thing, Bertrand, for you and Pigott. Shootings in the bosom of a family of distinction; a happy hunting-ground, combined with a happy home! Everything extra; all questions to be asked by the advertiser, and none answered by him; verified copy of pedigree to be forwarded, and sketch of armorial bearings. Capital! capital!"

"What does the fellow mean?"

"Listen"—and he read as follows:

"TO SPORTSMEN.—SHOOTINGS IN THE HIGHLANDS.—A gentleman of fortune and position, having rented for the ensuing season the celebrated shootings of Cairnarvoch, in the county of ———, which are too extensive for his requirements, in consequence of his having been disappointed of the partnership of his son and another gentleman, is willing to sublet shooting for two guns at £100 per gun. The MANSION-HOUSE OF CAIRNARVOCH is large and commodious, and having more accommodation than is required by the advertiser, he would be prepared to admit gentlemen sharing the shooting to a share also of the house; and as his establishment is on the handsomest scale, an arrangement might be made whereby the gentlemen (on terms hereafter to be agreed upon) should, to obviate the inconvenience of separate establishments, join his family circle; but in this case, as there are ladies of refinement in the family, the most satisfactory references as to position and character would be required. Application to be made to Messrs Buncombe & M'Nab, Solicitors, Gray's Inn, London."

"That sounds an odd sort of proposal," said Bertrand.

"To me it sounds very eligible," said another.

"How about the family circle, though?"

"Oh! that would be the best of it. Only read that advertisement; mark the suggested glories of the advertiser—his wealth, his social position, the size of his household, the refinement of his ladies—and say if it escapes your eagle eye that this man would be a mine of fun? and the ladies, Bertrand, think of *them;* if the shooting is only passable, *que voulez-vous?*"

"You seem to forget," said Pigott, "that *my* object *is* the shooting, not to trot out ridiculous old gentlemen, or to flirt with their daughters. One can do that here,—anywhere, —without the trouble and expense of a journey to the Highlands. The shooting must be much more than passable to satisfy *me*, I can tell you. Now I should not expect this shooting to be much; the man is in a hole, and wants to get out of it as cheaply as possible, small blame to him — but the whole thing smacks of 'Tommiebeg.' Does any one know anything about Cairnarvoch?"

"Know Cairnarvoch?" thundered M'Niven. "Ay, well I know it—paradise of sport; look you, a paradise. Grouse, capercailzie, ptarmigan, blue hares, black-game, and rabbits, woodcock, snipe, and roe, swarm on its hills and make the welkin black."

"Which being interpreted means that the shooting is first-rate?"

"All that the sporting heart desires. Too good, alack! if gouty hooves of pampered aldermen and the be-turtled——"

"Oh! spare us, spare us, Ossian: you can recommend the shooting, seriously?"

"On soul and conscience, Cameron, I can."

"Come, that alters the case," said Cameron.

"What do you think of it, Pigott? After all, the people won't matter much, if they give us plenty to eat and drink; open air all day and early hours at night; what do you say, Pigott?"

"I can't say anything about it till I've thought it over, talked it over, and smoked over it. I'm going to my quarters now: you can come if you like, and we'll do all three together." Whereupon the two friends left the mess-room.

As these two gentlemen are to play conspicuous parts in our story, it may here be as well to say something of them by way of introduction—albeit it is far from our intention to act the part of the master of ceremonies in the unsophisticated days of the drama, shouting, at each new entrance, "Here cometh in 'Spotless-Modesty'!" "Enter the 'Soul of Honour'!" "Listen to 'Refinement-of-Manners,'"—and so on. It is no part of our plan to thrust upon readers an inventory of all the vices and virtues, graces, adornments, specks, and flaws of each character at the outset, and so to send each character "on" with his *raison d'être* hung as a foregone conclusion about his neck.

Our *dramatis personæ* shall speak and act for themselves; and every one shall be at liberty to refer the deeds and words reported to such springs as may appear to each to be their legitimate sources. In this way the reader's right of private judgment shall not be filched from him, and this one reproach, at least, be avoided by the writer,

"Amphora cœpit
Institui; currente rotâ cur urceus exit?"

But as in everyday life, before presenting one person to another, we commonly, when we have the opportunity, furnish each with some slight *renseignements* of the other; so it will be convenient that we should say something by way of introduction to the personages who from time to time make their appearance on our little stage.

On this principle, let us introduce the two gentlemen who have retired for consultation; and first, Lieutenant Bertrand Cameron, of H.M.'s —th Regiment of Infantry. He was the only son of a gentleman of very ancient and distinguished family in the Scottish Highlands, who, in addition to a long yet authentic pedigree, had inherited a property not only magnificent in territorial extent, but yielding a revenue which, even according to Low-country standards, was magnificent. These combined advantages made the Laird somewhat of a *rara avis* in the Highlands; and it would have been well for him if he had been satisfied with that distinction; but it was not so. If his fortune was large, his ideas were on a much more extensive scale. He aspired to be a *rara avis* wherever he went. The prestige of his feudal grandeur in the north he supported in London and in Paris with a splendid recklessness; and what with that and the turf, and play, and an extravagant wife, and that *laissez-aller* easiness of disposition as to the state of his affairs, which marks its possessor as a sure prey for every class of marauder, a very few years had reduced the Laird to a state of desperate embarrassment. The nursing and retrenchment which might in time have restored the property was impossible to him; a run of luck at the tables, a fortunate *coup* on the turf,—such are the only resources which appear available to men of his disposition and training; and just at this time railway speculation, which was at its most frenzied height, offered him an obvious sandbank wherein to drop the mangled remains of his fortune. Of course he availed himself of it, and six months thereafter his property was brought to the hammer, and, followed by sincere regret, Mr Cameron disappeared from the social orbit in which he had been some time a particular star.

From a rental of £20,000 a-year nothing was saved—absolutely nothing. It was, indeed, fortunate that his wife had a few hundreds a-year in her own right; for on this pittance they had to depend entirely for subsistence, and on this they settled down in an obscure little town in France—to "make the best of it." When calamities of this sort come upon people well advanced in years, they have some consolation in feeling that they have had a long spell of the brighter side of life, and that, if the evil days have come at last, their duration cannot be very protracted; but here was a couple not yet near middle life, with a very short and very brilliant past behind them, and a very long and very dreary future in front, quite without hope of a change for the better. The prospect was too much for Mr Cameron. He "made the best of it" by declining to face the situation, and died in a few months of that mixture of regret, disgust, *ennui*, and despair which constitutes a very real and fatal disease, however much it may be sneered at when described as "a broken heart." His widow settled at Brussels with her only child Bertrand; but she did not very long survive her husband and her fortunes; and before he was ten years old Bertrand was an orphan, left to the guardianship of his uncle. This uncle was Roland Cameron, who, though the younger brother of his ward's father, had also inherited a very good property in the Highlands. The estate in question had been for centuries possessed by the Camerons; and though it was not entailed, it had been the family custom, by a system not uncommon in Scotland (which has been a fruitful source of litigation and hardship), that it should be held by him who, for the time being, was next in succession to the principal estate.

This system had, however, been abolished by Roland's father in his favour; he, in consideration, it was supposed, of the greatly-enhanced value of the first property, having devised to his second son absolutely the fee-simple of the second. Roland, although thus free from the usual hard conditions of younger sonship, had been endowed by nature with those qualities which frequently seem to compensate the cadet for the narrowness of his patrimony. He had intelligence, activity, perseverance, and energy —gifts which might have been allowed to waste themselves in inaction, wanting the spur of necessity, had it not been for his ambition, which was indomitable. This moved him to look about for a career with a wide horizon and large possibilities of eventual distinction, and he selected diplomacy as the profession in which he believed his talents would be most likely to find a suitable and congenial sphere.

Nor was he mistaken. His progress was more than usually rapid; and in consequence of a contribution which he made to the literature of an important international question, at a time when it was dividing political parties in England, he attracted the attention of the leaders of that party whose views he advocated. A seat was before long found for him in the House, and, once there, he soon talked himself —as so many have done before and since— into office. An under-secretaryship in a hard-worked department probably looks more desirable at a distance than from the point of view of an incumbent. Roland certainly found it so; and scarcely appreciated, as of the nature of a reward, the incessant application to laborious duties of routine which it imposed, or the official muzzle which forbade the free use of his versatile and discursive powers of talk. He gladly, therefore, when it came his way, accepted promotion to the governorship of a British dependency, which, although unimportant and not very remunerative, was the first step on the ladder by which he aspired to climb. Others were reached in due succession. He knew how to keep himself in the recollection of the Government and before the eyes of the public. If there was nothing stirring in his own particular colony, he was always ready with letters, articles, and pamphlets on the affairs of others. Sometimes his energy was of use, sometimes it was a bore; but either alternative conduces to advancement in the public service; and as each term of office expired, Roland was, as a matter of course, re-employed and promoted. At the time this story opens, he was governor of a most important colony in " Greater Britain ;" he had been made a K.C.B. ; and the value of his property in Scotland had been nearly trebled since his succession to it. Thus prosperity had hitherto shone upon him from every quarter. Up to this time there had been no check in his career ; and if it came now, as come it did, he had the melancholy satisfaction of feeling that he himself, and no such intangibility as Fortune, Fate, or the like, was to blame.

We all have our weak points, and it was in the point of morality that Sir Roland displayed a somewhat deplorable feebleness. The most servile of colonial courtiers could not have otherwise averred ; and in the fierce light which beats not merely on the throne, but on all governmental eminences, his Excellency's failings were conspicuously visible. Even in communities where the moral tone is not high, morality is exacted by public opinion from those who are set in authority—the reverse, at least, is always unpopular; and as Sir Roland, by successive promotions, came under the criticism of a larger and more civilised, and therefore more exacting, public opinion, his personal unpopularity increased. All his acts of government were accordingly criticised with an *animus* personally unfavourable to the Governor; and such as were unpopular in themselves were assailed with a vehemence and bitterness more than half-inspired by dislike to their originator. There was a turbulent legislature in Sir Roland's last and most important colony; a strong and vigorous party offered him a relentless opposition. Difficult questions of policy arose; and the good of the colony seemed at times a minor consideration with the Opposition compared with the defeat and humiliation of the Governor. His disposition, which was naturally haughty and autocratic, would not stoop to conciliation. He met the animosity of his opponents with fierce resentment; and in his measures of retaliation at last permitted himself to overstep constitutional limits. This at once embroiled him with friend and foe alike. The Imperial Legislature was appealed to, and Sir Roland found himself in danger of impeachment or of enforced retirement into private life. Thus matters stood with him at the opening of our tale; but we must not further anticipate his history.

At the time when young Bertrand was left to his guardianship he was still in a very minor colony, in a very remote part of the empire; and he at once arranged that the child's education should in the mean time be continued at Brussels; and having instructed his agent to select a suitable *pensionnat*, and establish his nephew at it, he troubled himself little more about his charge. Once annually he wrote the boy a letter, and once annually he received an answer—so that twice a-year he was certainly reminded that he possessed a nephew. Sir Roland (having been for many consecutive years absent from Europe) did not see Bertrand till he was fifteen years of age—

his last year having been spent at a military school in Germany. "The boy is growing up a confounded foreigner," was the verdict he pronounced on his young charge, in a tone of somewhat unreasonable displeasure. "We must get you home at once, youngster; and, by the by, what do you think of in the way of a profession?" Bertrand gave the answer which ninety young Britons out of a hundred would give at the same age. He unhesitatingly declared for the army; and his uncle making no objection, his future lot in life was thus summarily determined. He was at once transferred to Sandhurst, whence he was in due time gazetted to the —th Regiment, in which he had now served for five years—the two first with the depot of his corps in England and Ireland, and the remainder in that tropical station from which they had just returned at the opening of our story. It is only farther necessary to say something of Bertrand's personal appearance, which was extremely handsome and prepossessing; of that dark Celtic type which, with a clear complexion and grey hazel eyes, unites hair of the deepest and glossiest black. His features were refined and regular, the upper part of his face indicating bright intelligence; though perhaps the physiognomist might doubt, from symptoms of irresolution in the contour of the lower part of his face, and from the pattern of his mouth, whether this intelligence would not at times be scantily interpreted by his actions. A tall, lithe, active figure, the strength and symmetry of which were denoted by a singular grace, either in action or repose, completed a *tout ensemble* that would alike have delighted the eye of the artist and of the recruiting-sergeant. He was a favourite in his regiment; he had been a favourite at Sandhurst; and we need only farther add that we trust the reader's opinion of him may not altogether differ from that of his school-fellows and comrades. His friend Captain Watson Pigott was nobody's son in particular, and did not regret the circumstance in the least. If a man has a thorough respect for and appreciation of his own personal qualities, he is apt to undervalue family antecedents, particularly in these democratic days. He was four or five years older than Bertrand, and his personal appearance was neutral—eyes, mouth, hair, complexion, and height — all were neutral. Everything about him seemed to be devised to escape special remark; and, indeed, the only idea that occurred to one on first seeing him was, "What a clean-looking fellow!" But when you came to examine him more closely, from the cut of his hair and its faultless partition, down to his blameless boots, there was a quiet harmony in all his appointments that might lead one given to judge by externals to expect to find him a self-contained man, with a well-regulated mind.

His habits were not gregarious; indeed there was a certain *retenue* about his manner which was rarely laid aside, except in a *tête-à-tête*—and in *têtes-à-têtes* he almost never indulged except with Bertrand Cameron. His friendship for Bertrand, and his constant association with him, were perhaps the most salient points in his character in the judgment of his brother officers. They voted him a good-natured fellow, but suspected him of being intensely selfish, which may have arisen from the fact that he was rich, and yet not extravagant—a combination singularly grovelling and unlovely in the eyes of gentlemen whose meagreness of fortune was, as a rule, compensated for by a noble breadth of view as to the paternal relation in a pecuniary sense.

This will be sufficient as an introduction to the two young men whom we left retiring to consult on the Cairnarvoch question in Captain Pigott's quarters.

Bertrand Cameron, comfortably established in an arm-chair, with a cigar in his mouth, unfolded 'The Field' with solemn deliberation, and began to re-read the advertisement lately under discussion in the mess-room, approaching it with the air of one who has a knotty question to solve.

"I'll read it first, Pigott," he said; "then you shall read it, and then we'll compare notes and talk it over. It *will* require a deal of consideration, you know; we must do nothing in a hurry."

Bertrand's processes of thought must have been singularly rapid on this occasion, or his judgment arrived at altogether *per saltum;* for no sooner had he concluded the reperusal, than he jumped up with great vivacity, and thumping 'The Field' down on the table before Pigott, cried, "It's the very thing for us, Pigott—made for us, contrived for us—if we have only the luck to secure it. Let us write at once to these London lawyers and book it."

"I thought you had just said that it would require a deal of consideration?"

"So I thought, but I was mistaken. The second reading is everything: it gives one new lights, it opens fresh points of view; I see all the advantages of the plan now. Let's cry 'agreed,' and write to the lawyers."

"You forget I haven't had the advantage of a second reading yet."

"What a slow-coach you are! listen, then,"—and Bertrand again seized the paper and read the paragraph aloud, sonorously, enthusiastically, dwelling upon the points which he took to be most seductive, with the emphasis of a partisan.

"*Now*, what do you say, Pigott?" he cried, the reading concluded.

"My good man, what a hurry you're in!" replied his friend. "*You* may have inspirations — I haven't: give a fellow time to think."

"Well, well, what's your *primâ facie* view

of it? Hang it! You must have a *primâ facie* view of some sort; what is it?"

" Some one in the mess-room said it sounded like a 'Tommiebeg;' perhaps he was right. I shouldn't wonder if that was my *primâ facie* view, if I had time to discover it."

" Tommiebeg! humbug! It's well known to be one of the finest shootings in Scotland."

" So the advertisement says, of course; just as I, if I was advertising for a brigadiership in the American army, would likely describe myself as ' well known to be one of the finest soldiers in the British army.' Of course I should be speaking the truth; but the Yankees would scarcely engage me upon my own certificate, would they?"

" Well, M'Niven says it is true."

" M'Niven is an Ossian, not a Solomon."

" The game-book would show, at all events."

" Precisely; the first sensible words you've spoken in the matter, Bertrand. In the first instance, we should require to see the game-book."

" Well, let us write and ask for it, and engage the shooting conditionally on the book giving a satisfactory account."

"Ah! but there are other questions—the domestic, the financial."

"Well, what's your *primâ facie* view about them?"

"My *primâ facie* view about them is, that we have no means of taking any view of them whatsoever. Who is this 'gentleman of position'? who are his ladies of refinement? what does he define 'position' to be? and what is his notion of refinement? I confess to a certain inquisitiveness on these points—weak of me, perhaps, but I *am* a frail mortal. Then what is the entrance to his dress-circle to cost us? I am not a bloated aristocrat, as you know, and I don't think I'm a screw (though some asses say I am); but I must say I like to know my company, and I prefer to estimate the expense of a campaign before plunging into it."

"What a cautious old bloater you are! Talk of Scotchmen being 'canny'! Now look at yourself an Englishman, and at me a Scot; which of us two is the 'canny' one?"

"I sincerely believe and hope I am, Bertrand; but heaven forbid I should insult most grave and reverend Caledonia by considering a hare-brained lunatic like you a typical Scot!

but that isn't the question. I am a practical man, and I want to know what you've got to say to *my* questions."

"Oh! I detest a practical fellow; you've got no go, no dash, no spirit of adventure about you; but I know you're a mule, so pray take your own way, only take action of some sort at once. Remember this day fortnight is the 'Twelfth.'"

"Very well, Bertrand, I'll meet you in that, at all events. I'll write to Buncombe & M'Nab, and make them disgorge all essential particulars. You needn't be in such a state of mind —there's lots of time; all the world is not so impetuous."

"Sit down then, at once, and write."

And down Pigott sat and wrote accordingly; and, after some days, particulars were obtained sufficient to enable him to form at least "a *primâ facie* view" of the matter. Bertrand's fears were not realised. The shootings were still to be had. Nor were Pigott's "Tommiebeg" surmises substantiated, for the gamebook showed a really splendid average over the last five years.

The consideration to be paid for an entrance

to, and residence in, the domestic circle of Cairnarvoch, was pretty stiff—an " eye-opener," Pigott said; but Buncombe & M'Nab pledged their professional reputation that there would be ample equivalents, and Pigott thought he might surmount that objection. As to the social question, the lawyers said that the advertiser was a most esteemed client, a most respectable and wealthy gentleman—M'Killop by name, a native Scot, but who had spent all his life in the colonies, whence he had recently returned with a large fortune.

It was his intention to purchase a landed property in the north, for which he was on the look-out, and in the mean time he rented Cairnarvoch Castle. In reply to a half-expressed indication of surprise on Pigott's part that a gentleman of wealth and position should care to sublet his shootings, and admit total strangers into his family as a kind of boarders, the lawyers admitted that, though by no means without precedent, it might appear strange; but Mr M'Killop was a mercantile man, and mercantile men were apt to prefer the utilitarian to the conventional view of matters. Owing to the unexpected departure of his son and a friend for the colonies, he found himself with shooting on his hands three times as extensive as his requirements, and, as a man of business, he had resorted to the expedient in question. But it was not altogether by business motives that he was actuated. It would be a real benefit to him to have the society of some pleasant gentleman-like inmates; for a man, all his life in the colonies, found but few friends on his return home, and the district around Cairnarvoch had few residents, and at such distances as to render their society but little available.

The ladies of the family were three in number. Mrs M'Killop, her daughter by a former marriage, and Mr M'Killop's daughter, also by a former marriage, constituting, in the opinion of Messrs Buncombe & M'Nab, as truly charming a family circle as any gentleman could desire to be admitted to.

"It is something of a leap in the dark, Bertrand," said Pigott at last, after mature consideration of all these particulars; "but as there are a few streaks of light about it—the game average, for instance—I am prepared on the whole to take it. What say you?"

"What say I? what I said from the first; it's the very thing for us. We get rid of all the nuisance of servants and housekeeping, and stores and keepers and ghillies to look after, and a hundred other worries. We are certain of good sport, and if the society is not all we could wish, we can keep ourselves pretty much to ourselves. So it's agreed. Vive Cairnarvoch! Vive M'Killop! Vive Buncombe! Vive M'Nab! Vive everybody!"

All the arrangements were quickly completed, and ratified by an autograph letter from M'Killop, expressing his satisfaction, and describing their route; and on the morning of the 9th of August, behold our sportsmen starting from Euston Square by the Scotch mail, accompanied by Pigott's valet, a nondescript lad, in charge of the dogs, quite a small pack of setters, pointers, and retrievers, and all the usual *impedimenta* of sporting youths of condition.

CHAPTER II.

THE route by which Cairnarvoch was to be reached is one of the most delightful that can well be conceived—that is, after leaving Greenock, in which fetid and whiskyfied town our travellers found themselves at the close of their first day's journey. Here, rather than in Glasgow, they had resolved to sleep, so as to avoid an inconveniently early start on the morrow, when their journey was to be continued to Oban, in the far-famed steamer Iona.

Happy he or she who has yet to experience the first delights of that delectable voyage! and happier he or she who can look forward to repeating it, year by year, when summer days are fine! Given bright weather and a bright companion, the pleasure of that passage *is* something unique. The *mélange* of delights of which that steamer forms the nucleus is decidedly by itself,—and in this respect among others, that here almost every sort and condition of men must find some source of gratification and amusement.

"How?" "Why?" "What is there to do?"

You ask this, O *miseras hominum menteis?* —you ask this, O *pectora cæca*, that have never thrilled in unison with the pulsing of the Ionian paddle-wheels?

What is there to do? What is there not to do? and to see? First, if you have ever so little of an artist's eye or an artist's soul—that is to say, if you love nature at all—very surely you will find that love stirred and quickened within you all the live-long day—if you only keep your eyes open—while threading with the Iona the wondrous labyrinth of her beautiful course. The mountain panorama which greets you as you start, noble though it be, is but the noble promise of still better things; for it cannot show you the exquisite variety, the contrasts, the combinations, the marvellous chiaroscuro, the subtle harmonies, the sublime discords, that meet you and thrill you at every turn, passing through the inner penetralia of all that is most glorious in the land of mountain and of flood.

Gliding through those strange sounds and estuaries, with their infinite sinuosities, traced about peninsula and cape and island—traced as it were with a design of delighting the eye with sudden presentments of scenic surprises, as it were with a design of furnishing not one, but twenty points of view, wherefrom to consider each salient wonder and beauty round which they seem to conduct you proudly on their glittering paths—there must be something far wrong with you if you find no delight in all this. For here, indeed, you have a succession of the noblest pictures,—no mere iteration of rugged mountains, monotonous in their grim severity and sublime desolation,—no mere sleepy tracts of unbroken forest, nor blank heaths losing themselves vaguely in the horizon, nor undulating expanses of lawn-like pasture-land, but with something of all these features blending in each of the splendid series; every feature in turn claiming its predominance, when all the others seem to pose themselves about the one central object, sinking for the moment their own individualities that it may be glorified.

Something of this sort you may see at almost any point of the voyage; and then—as to what you may do—inspired by such scenes, you may well address yourself to

> "Feed on thoughts that voluntary move
> Harmonious numbers."

Or if inclined for a grosser sustenance, down below you will find the best and amplest means of satisfying such requirements. Or if tired awhile of ministering to the hunger of the soul, and of quelling the more sordid rage of carnal wants, you may look about you on the decks and cabins, and there find a rare opportunity of considering your kind in right humorous aspects.

We once heard a fellow-passenger remark, "This Iona is far better than most plays;" and he was very right. You won't often meet with a quainter assortment of human units. The steamer is a moving stage, on which you can see going on, side by side, no end of little dramas; and as for the *dramatis personæ*, who are they? or rather, who are they not?

Honeymooning couples huddled together under umbrellas to screen them from the sun, and from the world's garish eye; inevitable reading-parties from Oxford and Cambridge; indigestive blue-stockings, "inverted" philosophers, smug parsons, and leathery-looking lawyers; sportsmen *en route* for their shootings, yachting men for their yachts, gamekeepers, ghillies, and figure footmen; bleary Germans, and dyspeptic Yankees, calculating the exact number of cocked-hats into which the Mississippi knocks the Clyde; jocund schoolboys, bread-and-butter misses, "cock-lairds," and Cockneys; Highlanders and Mile-Enders; ladies and gentlemen,—all sorts and conditions of men, natural and artificial, shamming and detective, bragging and counter-bragging, appreciative and depreciative, a *farrago*, a *potpourri*, an *olla podrida*—a dainty dish to set before Democritus.

As these *personæ* shift about and interchange and intermingle, the scenes and acts of separate dramas get confused and entangled in the quaintest way. The hero of one walks into another and becomes its zany; and the high-life of a third suddenly appears cockaded and obsequious in a fourth. Look at two groups that are always to be seen on the Iona.

The first is ubiquitous—we meet it everywhere—the central figure being our old friend paterfamilias, with his semi-clerical look, his umbrageous "wide-awake," natty waterproof, guide-book, and eternal telescope. He is surrounded by his troop of rosy girls and smug youths, whom he dominates fussily. One of the boys has a contraband taste for tobacco, and preventive stratagems are in perpetual requisition. Another has an inquiring mind, and lurks dangerously about the engine-room. Then there is the waggish daughter — the female pickle—who never *can* see the particular point on which her papa desires to lecture; and the lackadaisical daughter, who requires constant rousing from her novel to contemplate the book of nature ; and the mysterious female friend with a look of chronic sea-sickness ; and the limp mamma, with a headache and slight infirmity of temper which requires coaxing. All these cares and troubles are on the shoulders of poor paterfamilias, and yet he contrives to explain everything to everybody who approaches. Who has not met this group at all sorts of places ? Who has not seen this typical family tourist, with his fussy look of abnormal relaxation ? But does any one " know him at home " ? What is he ? What does he do, and where does he do it, when he is not panting up the Righi, or expatiating at Ramsgate, or ogling the Rhineland ? Does any one know him ? or will Mr Pollaky undertake to run him to earth ?

Down below in the cabin we have another group inevitable in the Iona, but not much met with elsewhere. It is a small tradesman's family from Glasgow " oot for a bit jant."

In this case the head of the family separates himself from his kith and kin, and keeps holiday independently in the fore-cabin. How he has amused himself we have a fair opportunity of judging at the conclusion of the voyage, when (but not till then) he emerges from his lair, solemn, sodden, staggery, with imbecile up-liftings of the arms and monotonous inarticulate murmurs, as who would preach—and without doubt that is what he is attempting to do; for, say what they like of " our own flesh and blood " in Scotland, their festal programme, simple though it be, is not absolutely fulfilled by whisky—a little theology is supposed to give " bite " and relish to the " barley bree." His " sonsy " wife remains mistress of the group in the saloon. It is large enough, luckily, to contain many groups, but hers is the most notable. She sits there in company with seven children, two quart bottles of milk, a soda-water bottle filled with a pellucid liquor, a paper containing some glutinous sweetmeat, a basket of gooseberries, another basket which is covered with a cloth, but emits pungent odours as of cheese. The youngest child is, of course, in arms; it is teething before our very eyes, and is obviously the victim of intestinal pangs. It cries incessantly when it is not being nourished, and when it *is* nourished (in open court) it chokes. The other children, who appear to be *all* about five years old, play, romp, fight, scream, yell, finally are whipped in the old-fashioned style, with much preliminary untrussing of points.

Certain spinsters flounce from the saloon, a nervous fellow is *agacé* and swears, a coarse fellow laughs aloud. What does *she* care, this notable woman ? She has paid her fare and will take her ease : " The baby canna dee o' hunger, and the bairns *maun* hae their skelps. Afore folk ? Whatna folk ? Cock *them* up." Accept these specimens, and then call up how whimsically in contrast all this sort of thing is to the scenery through which the steamer is gliding—scenery ever varying, unchanging only in its one fidelity to the beautiful and the sublime.

Oh, dear reader, we have ridden thus long on our Ionian hobby, and very likely we have bored you. But if you, too, are an Ionian, forgive our tediousness, appreciating our zeal; whereas if the Iona is still an untasted joy, accept our prolixity as a chastening and penal visitation, and next summer supply the missing experience.

On board this steamer, and surrounded by some such accessories as those above sketched, behold our two travellers embarked on the tenth morning of August—the brightest month of the Scottish year. Pigott's tastes as a devoted sportsman had frequently brought him to Scotland before, but it was Bertrand's first visit to the land of his sires. This (unacknowledged) circumstance was a secret and rankling source of grief and shame to him—that he, the scion of a thousand sons of the heather (not to speak of the mist), should never yet have planted his chieftain foot upon his ancestral hills, seemed to him to be indeed a woe and a disgrace to be carefully concealed; and his desire on this occasion to guard the secret from his companion cost him no small efforts of self-restraint and of finesse. Sore, indeed, was the trial to curb manifestations of excessive enthusiasm, which might suggest non-familiarity with Scottish scenery, and to repress eager questions which were for ever rising to his lips. Had his companion been as demonstrative a man as himself, his task would have been simpler; but Pigott was essentially of the "*nil-admirari*" school — surprise, admiration, excitement of any sort, appeared to be contraband of his mental laws, insomuch that any commendatory remarks elicited from him by a first view of Niagara or the Matterhorn would have differed but little in form and tone from his favourable verdict on the freshness of his egg at breakfast, or some extra radiance in the polish of his boots. Bertrand's secret had, of course, been fathomed by him, and he circled round and round it in his conversation, to the confusion of his friend and his own cynical amusement at the boyish absurdity.

But Bertrand had another cause of disquiet. With some palpitations of the heart he had that morning determined to array himself for the first time in the "garb of Old Gaul:" when, however, he had laid out the different parts of the dress (which had been supplied by a London tailor), a difficulty arose. A South-Sea islander of average intelligence might probably enough contrive without instruction to get himself inside a pair of trousers; but any one of us would find it a hard task to array himself in the beads, paint, feathers, and other paraphernalia of the savage, so as to pass muster as a gentleman-like, well-dressed cannibal of fashion: and so in a minor degree is it with the Highland dress. Poor Bertrand looked at the kilt and could find no visible means of fastening it. In despair he essayed to gird it on with a portmanteau-strap worn *en ceinture;* but its dimensions were hopelessly voluminous, and he came to the mournful conclusion that he must have been accidentally supplied with a dress intended for some masquerading London alderman of especial obesity.

What was to be done? Time was flying. Must he relinquish his intention of entering the Highlands as a Cameron, glittering in the proud plumage of a mountain bird? Perish the thought! He would try very diplomatically to get a wrinkle from the waiter, whom he summoned accordingly. "Oh, waiter, I find I've got some one else's kilt sent with me by mistake; it's miles too large, and I wanted to see if you could contrive any dodge for tucking it in, so that I might wear it for the day. I hate travelling in trousers; and, by the by, there's nothing to fasten it with. I never saw such a kilt in my life."

The waiter, a stolid-looking West-Highlander, examined the garment, and then gave an inquisitive semi-comical glance at its would-be wearer. "I'll sort it for you, sir," he said; and in a twinkling the refractory garment was wrapped round Bertrand's loins and pinned with two big pins about the haunch and hip-joint. "There, sir, it'll no be getting lowse noo," he promised, when the investiture was completed. He then helped Bertrand to "do on" the sporran, hose, brogues, skien-dhu, &c. &c., to which our Celtic novice, in his innocence, added a belted plaid, brooch, and dirk. All that was metallic in his appointments was of silver, freely incrusted with rampagious cairngorms; and altogether his appearance was as gorgeous as the most florid taste could desire.

Thus equipped, with his bonnet (bearing a huge silver platter of armorial devices, and an eagle's plume) cocked jauntily on his right ear, Bertrand descended in mingled pride and perturbation to the coffee-room, where Pigott was alreaded seated at breakfast. He posed himself serio-comically at the door to disarm the cynic by meeting him half-way. His friend looked at him and munched, and looking and munching, his eyes got a trifle larger, and at last, with a ghost of a grin, he remarked, " In the name of the Prophet, how did you get into that thing?"

"If you mean the Highland dress," said Bertrand, flaring up at once, "I got into it, I suppose, as other Highlanders have done."

"One can conceive no limits to the eccentricities which other Celts may have performed, especially in their cups. Brian O'Lynn, for instance, had his coat buttoned behind, and turned inside out."

"And pray what has that got to do with me and my dress?"

"Only that you've been following in the Irish Celt's wake in putting your kilt on hindside in front."

"Pshaw! nonsense!"

"I'll prove it; sit down."

Bertrand flounced himself down on a chair, and the heavy sporran swinging aside, up sprang the kilt in front, the plaits that should have been behind fanning themselves out like a peacock's tail. Up started Bertrand. "There *must* be something wrong, I suspect."

"I have something more than a suspicion to the same effect," rejoined Pigott. "Go and take it off; I wouldn't run the gauntlet of the Iona with a fellow rigged like that for a trifle."

"It's a new kind of kilt," faltered Bertrand; "but I'll get accustomed to it. I won't take it off."

"Oh, if you're obstinate, at least let me put it on right for you. I flatter myself I know all the eccentricities of the garment. I used to wear it deer-stalking when I was young and foolish."

Here was a humiliation for the *de jure* mountaineer; but it was obviously necessary to get on a better understanding with his garments before starting, so he crept meekly upstairs with Pigott, remarking, " It's wonderful how soon one gets out of the trick of a dress of that sort."

Two chamber-maids and the waiter looked out of a room as they passed, and retired sniggering violently, and Bertrand ground his teeth with rage as he recognised, and promised himself a future revenge for, the trick which the rascal had played him. After the kilt had been adjusted, Pigott persuaded him to tone down the rest of his appearance by suppressing plaid, brooch, dirk, and other superfluities; so that when he appeared on the quarter-deck of the Iona, barring that his unsunned knees were of a dazzling whiteness, that his jacket was velvet, and his kilt of full-dress tartan, there was nothing radically amiss with him in his quality of *montagnard*.

He was, as we have said, a very handsome fellow; and as he and his friend commenced their promenade on deck, he was quite a central object of observation, which was rather embarrassing at first, and every now and then suggested grave suspicions of the conduct of his kilt, which he felt to be a garment of terrible possibilities. But by degrees his self-consciousness was quieted down, and he was able to look the world boldly enough in the face. Of course the steamer contained the usual quaint groups and *outré* individuals; and as our travellers moved about among them, they found ample sources of amusement. Pigott, walking up and down with that abstracted air which seems to imply a consciousness of no other presence than the wearer's own, contrived, by a few rapid, sidelong glances, to take in the various humours of the scene, and fell to expounding *sotto voce* to his companion the conditions and characteristics of their fellow-voyagers, telling them off in short epigrammatic sentences. "Why, Pigott," he exclaimed, when a temporary cessation took place on their arrival at one of the numerous landing-stages, "you would make your fortune as a showman; but what an ill-conditioned ruffian you must be! you haven't got a good word to say for any of them."

"Why should I? I don't know any good of any of them; and even if I had said anything bad of any of them—which I deny—in groping for the truth it is always best to err on the safe side."

"And the safe side is to make them all out bad?"

"Well, for choice, I should say so decidedly; but I have done nothing of the sort; I have only pointed out their actual or possible absurdities."

"How would you like to be laughed at yourself?"

"Like it? of course I like it. I *am* laughed at, so are you, so is everybody, by some one or other. I laugh at a man for what I consider his absurdities; he believes in himself, and is all the while laughing at me for my ridiculous deficiency of the very qualities I deride in him. We are both pleased. We are all Ishmaelites in the matter of mirth. The doctrine is a great comfort to me. It teaches me that I violate no Christian precept—at all events, I do as I know I *am* done by."

"Yes, but every one doesn't think as you do. I don't go in for laughing at people myself, and I know I should hate being laughed at—not that I suppose there *is* much to laugh at about me, and I don't suppose I *am* laughed at. Should you?"

"Candidly, I should certainly say you are; and still more candidly, I should say you deserve it; that kilt, for instance——"

Bertrand stopped abruptly, and hurriedly examined the hinder portion of the garment, with a renewed terror that it was repeating its peacock manœuvre in rear.

"Oh! bother the kilt. Don't let us prose! What a charming place! What a crush of people! but half your oddities are going out. Why, they're all leaving; look!"

"Never mind, they will be replaced: the tide has just done ebbing, and here it comes flowing again." And truly the departing crowd were soon replaced by one similar in quantity and quality.

On they came, crushing breathless and eager along the gangway, with a brandished forest of walking-sticks, umbrellas, camp-stools, baskets, and so on—the Captain on the paddle-box looking like Noah passing his cargo into the ark.

"Holloa!" cried Bertrand, suddenly. "What's this?"

"Where?" asked Pigott.

"Why, there, on the pier, just coming in."

"Oh," said Pigott, "that's a very nice point for consideration; don't hurry me. Not Helen M'Gregor—she's too old for that; nor Madge Wildfire, nor Meg Merrilies, nor Norna of the Fitful Head; she has a dash of all four, but—— No, I give her up."

The subject of these remarks was a tall, plethoric, elderly lady, in whose attire and complexion all the colours of the rainbow, and a good many more, met in a blaze of inharmonious combinations. A bright silk-tartan dress, involving stripes of the most contradictory tints, was surmounted by a black velvet tunic, over which was draped a shawl of another tartan—differing in all, save its variegated brilliancy, from the dress. A huge cairngorm brooch fastened the shawl under her chin, but its lustre paled before the superior brilliancy of the ample round red face, which wibbled and wobbled in its billowy fatness above.

Great ogreish teeth flashed from a ravine

bisecting the lower part of this ruddy orb. Two pale twinkling eyes, seeming for ever about to set behind high but full-fleshed cheek-bones, peered over a short up-turned nose; while above, a profusion of grizzled flaxen hair towered in fantastic coils, detaching one perfectly inauthentic ringlet to patrol the capacious shoulders. The whole edifice was crowned by a perky white bonnet, from which, as from a festive May-pole, streamed many a banneret of tartan ribbon.

This wondrous creature, posed in an attitude of command, stood looking down on the quarter-deck and its inhabitants, as if doubting their worthiness to be admitted to a closer contact with herself, and probably to give them an unobstructed view of the glory which was about to descend into their midst. But the steamer had embarked its passengers, the "dreadful bell" had jangled thrice, and the Captain, in that state of normal fuss and "boilover" which belongs to his tribe, having shouted irreverently to the lady to "come along if she was coming," the paddle-wheels began to make some premonitory revolutions. Thus stimulated, and followed by a young lady and a maid of spectral aspect, who looked as if her substance and colour had been absorbed into the luminary of which she was the satellite, the great being moved heavily across the gangway, sending Parthian shafts back to a couple of porters, who were staring with incredulous contempt at certain minute coins in their extended palms with which she had just failed to satisfy them.

Leaning on the maid, she sailed up the quarter-deck with a backward rake of the head; and, after a world of fussy arrangements of rug and shawl, came to an anchor in a prominent situation, and proceeded to "take stock" of her fellow-passengers haughtily, through a massive double eye-glass.

The effect upon them of this *entrée* was varied.

"Mair like a muckle plei-actress nur a dacent wummin," soliloquised an acid Glasgow matron, withdrawing her teeth from the recesses of a bun to make the remark.

"Oh, goot life!" snivelled a delighted Celt at her elbow, "but she put the fear o' deas on the pit porter podies."

"Whew!" whistled Pigott, "Solomon in

all his glory could have been nothing to this."

"I rather think, sir," said an ever-hovering paterfamilias who overheard the remark, and was, as usual, ready to supply information of the most dilapidated description,—"I rather think she is a chieftainess."

"She looks like one, don't she?" said Pigott.

"She does indeed, sir; and if my memory carries me aright—a relative of the Duke of Argyll's."

"I shouldn't wonder: he *has* a few relatives in these parts, I believe."

"Yes, and I really believe she must be *the* lady who owns several of the Hebrides; a very noble-looking person; so national, eh?"

"Oh! decidedly so," &c. &c. &c.

There was as strong as possible a contrast between the appearance and equipments of the chieftainess and those of the young lady who accompanied her. The only bright colours which adorned the latter were to be found in the rosy bloom of her cheek, and in the golden sheen which rippled through the deep masses of her auburn hair. Her face was a most pleasing one; and if it was deficient in that severe regularity of feature which painters and sculptors are perversely supposed to desiderate, there was a frank, fresh, joyous simplicity looking out of her bright hazel eyes, and a genial kindliness about her whole expression, which might perhaps be more likely to win hearts worth winning than the most chiselled perfection of outline and proportion. Her height, though looking insignificant beside the colossal dimensions of her companion, was in reality above the average; and her figure, light, active, and graceful, was set off to advantage in a close-fitting tunic and simple skirt of a neutral colour.

The course of the great woman's inspection soon brought her to Pigott and Cameron, and she favoured them with a very protracted scrutiny, dwelling chiefly upon Bertrand, over whose equipments her eyes promenaded with looks of curious disapprobation. That foolish fellow found himself getting very red and uncomfortable. To be narrowly inspected by any one would have been embarrassing enough at the moment; but to be weighed in the balance and found Celtically wanting by a chieftainess "to the Highlands bound" was woe indeed.

Presently she turned to her companion and made some remark which caused the young lady to glance quickly in the direction of the two young men; and then a short conversation followed which they partially overheard.

"I'm certain it's them," said the elder lady. "Go and find out."

"Find out!" laughed the girl. "How? am I to go and ask them?"

"Ask the Captain."

"But the Captain is not the least likely to know."

"Go and ask him."

"Oh, please don't ask me to go. I should never be able to struggle through all these dreadful men on the paddle-boxes. And surely there is no serious hurry: if these are the gentlemen, we are sure to know in plenty of time; and if not, it won't signify who they are."

"Salfish! parvarse! as usual I must go mysalf;" whereupon she rose and moved down the quarter-deck.

Presently she had got hold of one of the men of the steamer; and after some conversation, of which Bertrand and Pigott could perceive that they were the subjects, they saw her conducted to the stack of luggage, saw her halted in front of theirs, saw her deliberately read the labels thereon, and return in triumph to her companion, remarking, " I was right—it *is* them ; I'll go and speak to them."

" Oh, please not," said the younger lady.

" Why not, pray ? "

" It looks so forward and inquisitive ; and they must have seen you reading their addresses."

" Affectation ! I have no patience with you;" and she turned and advanced upon Bertrand and Pigott. But Pigott, divining her intention, and remarking to his friend, " Without doubt a Highland kinswoman of yours, who recognises the family knee, and is coming to rend us," they broke and fled to the paddle-boxes, and there remained in safety till the vessel reached Ardrishaig, where disembarkation is necessary to cross by the Crinan Canal to the Iona's sister on Loch Crinan.

On their walk up to the Canal they overtook and passed the ladies. " Now, then," they heard the elder say, " I've got them ; ahem ! "

"No, no!" whispered the younger lady.

"I will; ahem! ahem! ahem!" and the latter sounds being obviously intended to attract their attention, Bertrand and Pigott turned round and were at once accosted by their pursuer. Her accent was extremely Scotch, and a grotesque attempt to veneer it with the tones of the Southron, and to gild it with a few French phrases, made her all but unintelligible. We shall only attempt in her first few sentences to represent the hideous sounds of which she was guilty.

"Meal perdong, jontlemen!" she exclaimed—"dee meal perdong! a little burrd has whispered to me that you are ong root for Cairnarvoch; was the little burrd correct?"

Pigott replied that the bird's intelligence was accurate, with an involuntary glance in the direction of the younger lady, as if surmising that she was alluded to under the metaphor.

"Let me," continued the chieftainess, "jontlemen, let me introjooce you to my daughter, Miss Grant."

The two young men made their obeisances in great bewilderment.

"The little burrd," continued the chieftainess, archly, "has told me something else."

"Indeed?"

"Yes, indeed—your names."

"The little bird seems to take a very flattering interest in us."

"Yes: you are Captain Pigott, neyspau?"

"I am indeed."

"And you," turning to Bertrand, "are Mr Cameron, neyspau?"

"The bird seems to be infallible."

"I could tell that you were intended to be a Cameron by your tartans, of course. Well, jontlemen, I'm deloited to make your acquointance, I'm shaw." The party then moved on together, the two young men much puzzled as to who this oracle might be who stopped them on the Queen's highway to tell them who they were and whither they were going.

"We are most fortunate in our weather," remarked Bertrand.

"We are," replied the lady, eyeing him grimly all over; "and that, let me say, is very fortunate for your jacket—a velvet jacket—a silk-velvet jacket!—you must excuse me for saying that it has a peculiar look in the morning."

"I am sorry to hear it," said Bertrand, blushing painfully.

"Yes," continued the lady, "out of all taste. How would I look in a silk-velvet gown on board a steamer?"

"There can be no question that the effect would be superb in any situation," said Pigott, gravely, coming to the rescue of his friend.

"Which shows that *you* know nothing about it," rejoined the chieftainess, ignoring the compliment. "Full-dress tartan, too! it is very suspicious—very."

"I trust you don't suspect me of being an accomplice, madam," said Pigott, gravely.

"I know nothing about you, but my suspicion is that he is only a Cockney Highlander after all."

"No, I'm not, indeed; I'm as Highland as—as—anything."

"As a peat, you would have said, if you had been *pure song*."

"To confess the truth, then, though I am *pur sang* a Highlander, I know nothing of the language, I am ashamed to say."

"That's honest, at all events; and, if you *are* a Highlander, we must teach you up at

Cairnarvoch to look like one, and to speak the language, and how to dance strathspeys and reels and Ghillie Callum, and toss the caber, and throw the hammer, and eat haggis, and drink whisky and Athole brose, and——"

"I am afraid it would take too long to teach me so many desirable accomplishments—that is, if I am to shoot any grouse; but am I to understand that we are to have the happiness of being your neighbours at Cairnarvoch?"

"Neighbours! why, aren't you coming to stay with us?"

"Ah! really—too kind—but——"

"Mamma, you quite forget that these gentlemen can't possibly know who you are," said Morna.

"And why not, pray?"

"Unless they have the 'second-sight.'"

"You are forgetting yourself, Morna. Is this so, jontlemen? Am I not known to you?"

"A little bird," said Pigott, "has whispered to me that you are Mrs Grant."

"That's right and wrong."

"She must have been drinking before she came on board," thought both the men.

"Right, because I *was* Mrs Grant; wrong because I'm not."

"Fearfully intoxicated," thought Pigott and Bertrand—"a painful spectacle."

"I see, in introjoocing my daughter I forgot myself. She is Miss Grant, my daughter by my *first*, Captain Grant; but I am now Mrs M'Killop, to whose house you are going." The young men expressed due satisfaction at the discovery, and she went on loftily: "The mistake is tickling; but one is so accustomed to be known in one's own country by every one, that it does not occur to one that one is not known by any one."

"It was deplorable stupidity on our part," said Pigott, "and we beg to apologise."

"We'll say no more about it," said the lady, with magnanimity; "we were staying with some friends on a visit at Port Maikie; but I harrd two days ago from M'Killop that you were to arrive to-day, so we have returned to receive you; and here we are at the Canal and the steamer. Captain Pigott, kindly give me your hand up the ladder; Morna, take my parasol; M'Kenzie (to the spectre), run up and prepare a seat. Let me give you a hint,

Mr Cameron, in ascending the ladder to be very careful. You look like a fish out of water in that dress; and an Englishman in a kilt is usually a shocking, indecent sight."

"I shall certainly spare you such an infliction," said Bertrand, in a rage. "I shall stay below. Pigott, you will find me in the cabin when you come down again."

"It is a wise plan," rejoined the matron, "for the sun will soon have blistered these poor white knees of yours—I can see that; and you will avoid impertinent remarks at the same time, which your appearance provocks. It would be unpleasant to have every one saying, 'Who in the world is *this* with Mrs M'Killop?'—would it not?"

"Very much so indeed; but you need have no fear of my compromising you—or myself." And Bertrand, torn with rage and mortification, increased by the tittering of some bystanders who overheard Mrs M'Killop's loud remarks, flounced into the little cabin and sat down in a corner, thankful for the small mercy of finding it empty.

Presently he was joined by his friend.

"Well, Bertrand," said he, " even you are laughed at sometimes, it seems."

"Yes," roared Bertrand, starting up; "but it's the last time I shall be laughed at for this infamous dress. It *is* a savage dress, an abominable contrivance of the foul fiend. I'll change it directly I get to Oban; and as for that she-savage, I wish she was overboard."

"I think she is rather a trump—mad, of course, but a trump."

"I admire your taste. This is one of your 'ladies of refinement' you've let me in for."

"Come, come, Bertrand, you're unreasonable."

"Not a bit of it; it was all your doing. You brought me here, but hang me if I stay here! I'll give up my leave and go back to-night—I tell you, to-night."

"In trousers, of course?" suggested Pigott.

"In trousers! I should rather think so."

While Bertrand was indulging in this childish ebullition below, the cause of his ire was being taken to task on deck. "Mamma," said Miss Grant, when Pigott left them, "what could induce you to be so rude to Mr Cameron?"

"I protest I don't understand you, gurl; I never was rude in my life."

"You told him he was a Cockney, that his dress was out of taste and ridiculous, and that it was unpleasant to you to be seen with him. It has hurt his feelings, at all events, whether it was rude or not, and made me feel—feel——"

"Oh, out with it; say it at once. You're ashamed of your mother—that's it; and this is what comes of your fine education, and living with your mother's enemies; this is the Grant spirit—quite the Grant spirit—most undutiful!"

"Mamma, you know I would rather be anything than undutiful; but surely you can't wish to say unkind things to people, or to hurt their feelings intentionally; and if I see you doing it without being aware, it can't be undutiful of me to tell you."

"You are far too fond of lecturing. I saw this young man had a high look and a conceited manner, and I thought it my duty to put him in his place at once. Who is he? Some beggarly subaltern, who thinks, because he pays us a rent, that we are to be the dust under his feet! No, no; I've put him in his place, and in his place I'll keep him. He may be the son of a London shopkeeper for all we know."

"Well, mamma, I declare I saw nothing the least assuming or impertinent about either of these two gentlemen; and surely it would be time enough to put them in their places when they become so."

"I beg *your* pardon. We have too many of these sham Highlanders nowadays. It is most offensive to the old blood."

"You don't know that this gentleman is not of the old blood."

"What! and travel in a silk-velvet jacket and full-dress tartan?—preposterous!"

"At any rate, whoever he is, he certainly did nothing to offend you, and I am afraid you have certainly offended him. Is this Highland hospitality?"

"No one can say a word against my hospitality; and if you really think the poor creature takes to heart so much what I said, I'll put him at his ease again in a moment. I have tact."

This valuable quality she put in requisition

on Bertrand's reappearance, which, however, did not take place till they were approaching the end of the voyage. Then advancing to him with a subtle smile in her pig's eyes, she peered into his dark countenance, and remarked mincingly, " Gloomy, gloomy face ! " —an exhibition of tact which, though twice repeated, had not the instantaneous effect expected; on the contrary, Bertrand showed symptoms of retreat.

" A high temper is a sad curse, Mr Cameron," she continued. " I see you suffer from it; but if I had known its violence, my playful rub would have been spared. No person of tact would wantonly infuriate such a disposition."

To be grossly insulted, and then accused of having a furious temper because he had simply avoided his insulter, struck Bertrand as rather strong, and he replied with a dignified falsehood, " You must pardon me if I am quite at a loss to understand your allusions."

"Oh, don't attempt to deny it. In my playful way (I'm a sad joker) I rallied you about your dress, which is, you must feel, a little *bazarre*, and about your white limbs, and so forth, and you must needs fly into a tantrum and shut yourself up in the cabin, foaming and swearing, I've no doubt. It's choildish, choildish; we must all bear rubs, and to show temper to a lady is not, let me tell you, commy faw in a Highland gentleman, which seems to be the character you aim at !!"

"I flatter myself, madam, it is the character which I have the honour to possess," said Bertrand, loftily.

"Ah! perhaps, perhaps; but silk velvet in the morning, and a dress tartan—you must see that these are very suspicious."

"I don't really know what you suspect me of," cried Bertrand, bursting, in spite of himself, into a laugh at this singular moral and social criterion.

"That's right; another laugh, and the black dog will be off your back. It is suspicious, as I said. You see we have many London Cockneys coming down here dressed out like you, and we don't like it; the old blood doesn't like it: right or wrong, it is insulting to the old blood."

"You imply that I am one of the London Cockneys?"

"No, I didn't say *imply*. I said that there was a suspicious look about the whole thing."

"Then let me relieve you by saying that I believe in this very district there is no blood older than mine."

"Ah! yes, it's common to say that, and believe it too, I daresay; but when one comes to investigate,—to say, 'Show me your ruins, your tombs, your castles passed away to strangers and Sassenachs,'—there is often a hitch—a hitch."

"I daresay we can show tombs and ruins with our neighbours; as to castles passed away to Sassenachs, I am glad to say there *is* a hitch; but there is a castle in this county belonging to us, and I believe it has been some five hundred years in our possession. I had a notion that *that* made us a pretty old family; but if it is necessary to sell it before we can be recognised as 'the old blood,' I hope we shall continue *parvenus* of the fourteenth century."

"It is a fair age, certainly," said the lady, "though nothing to the M'Whannels, my maternal ancestors; but there is no family answering to all this except the Camerons of

Aberlorna, and there is only one old man in it."

"There you are mistaken; there is also a young one, and I am the individual."

"The relationship will be pretty distant, I'm thinking."

"Not so very far off; I am Sir Roland Cameron's nephew."

"His nephew?"

"Yes."

"Dear, dear! how stupid of me! Then you must have been an orphan?"

"I still am, unfortunately."

"And you didn't die, as was said, at the same time as your parents?"

"So it would seem."

"Oh! this is all very different—gratifying, indeed," exclaimed Mrs M'Killop, with enthusiasm; "we'll shake hands, if you please, and think no more of my little rub, which could never apply to a Cameron of Aberlorna. Satirical people like me are often led away into saying things they don't mean; and if your dress *is* a little fine, his most sacred Majesty George the Fourth landed at Leith in full dress, which ought to be a setting of the fashion; and it will be a pleasure to me to receive you into our house. Indeed it's a kind of revival of old times, for there is a connection between us."

"Really?"

"Yes; although there has been no intercourse and something more than a coolness between the families for generations, there *is* a connection. You must have heard of Tork M'Ouanall, who received thirty-seven wounds —all mortal—at the battle of Inverlochy?"

"I'm afraid not."

"No? how droll! well, he was my ancestor, and he married a Cameron (it was a great match for the Camerons, although I say it), and that makes the connection."

"It is the proudest moment of my existence," said Bertrand, his ill-humour vanishing at the absurdity of the whole scene.

"Morna, you must shake hands with Mr Cameron," said her mother.

Morna gave a look of half-annoyance, with which, however, fun was struggling, and held out her hand to Bertrand, who gallantly remarked, "Let the *vendetta* of generations die from this hour."

"A most extraordinary coincidence, I must say," continued Mrs M'Killop, "that we should become acquainted in this way. We are very clannish, we Highlanders, Captain Pigott; and I daresay you can scarcely understand the feelings of delight which Mr Cameron and I are enjoying just now?"

Pigott confessed that, though enviable, they *were* a trifle beyond his depth; and here the voyage, like the *vendetta*, came to a close, and any hope our travellers might have cherished of escaping from the toils of their hostess were at once dispelled by her remarking, "M'Killop has arranged that we are all to dine here together, and drive home in the evening. He was to bespeak all necessary conveyances for the joint party."

"A charming plan," said Pigott; "and what is the length of the drive?"

"From three to four hours; but it is never dark at this season, and we shall all be refreshed by the cool jews."

Before long they were seated at an excellent dinner in the hotel, and its soothing influence very soon told upon the party. Bertrand forgot his sulks, his annoyances, even his kilt;

and his heart was merry within him, as he sat amicably *vis-à-vis* to the descendant of the ill-fated Tork.

As for that lady, after a glass or two of champagne, she became more than ever communicative, pouring forth, in an unbroken stream, choice extracts from her personal and family history.

It was thus that our travellers became aware that her maiden name had been M‘Kechnie (which was not to be confounded with M‘Kechran or M‘Fechnie, these being inferior septs), a clan of unusual antiquity and power, but which, surprising as it might seem, was not to her so great a source of pride as her descent maternally from the M‘Whannels. Pigott gravely assented that he *was* scarcely prepared for *that*. It was true, however, she averred; but all their grand days were over. Clans and clansmanship were at an end. Their properties had passed to aliens. The M‘Kechnies were landless as the Gregarach; and, to his undying disgrace, the titular chief of the M‘Whannels was content to supervise the excise department of his native district for the meanest of stipends.

Washing away ancestral sorrows with a glass of champagne, Mrs M'Killop came to her own personal history, and explained that in their reduced state the daughters of her clan could not afford to be fastidious in matrimonial matters. Hence her marriage, contracted in spite of personal advantages which she need not dwell upon (but did, however, at great length), with Grant, a worthy man, and a cadet of a good house, but only a "marching captain." He died, and she had sorrowed for him —honestly and conscientiously mourned him— as long as was fit and proper, whatever a set of stuck-up vinegar old maids might say to the contrary; "after whom" (with a fierce glance at Morna) "she hoped no daughter of hers would take,"—a remark which brought the young lady into action, her annoyance at her mother's absurdity being no longer repressible, and she said: "Mamma, I don't think our family matters can be very amusing to these gentlemen, and I do beg of you, at all events, to say nothing against my dear, kind aunts; you know how it vexes me."

"There!" said Mrs M'Killop, looking round at the two gentlemen,—"there it is. This comes of living with aunts. Poor Grant had a fancy that this child should spend half her time with his sisters, and this is what comes of it—temper and insubordination which only a mother's tact and tuition could control. I will say nothing more of *your* friends, Morna, since it is unpleasant to you; but I will go on with my little story, as I take leave to think it will interest these gentlemen, both of whom are to be our inmates, and one of whom is in a manner connected." And this brought her to her marriage with M'Killop, a gentleman who had, a few years before, returned from the colonies. He had realised everything there, and resolved upon the purchase of an estate in Scotland, where, by a strange coincidence, his clan had also become as landless as any M'Kechnie or M'Whannel of them all. By another coincidence, M'Killop was a widower, with one son and one daughter. When he had urged his suit, which he had done with a very proper importunity, she had carefully weighed everything; and her daughter's interests being paramount, the circumstance that he, too, had a daughter, had told in his favour. "The companionship will be good for my child," she had said; "I will be a mother to his girl, he a father to mine;" and so had yielded. "I have not repented my decision," she continued; "like Auld Robin Gray, M'Killop has been 'a kind man to me.'" And she spoke as though the wedding had involved sacrifices on her part equivalent to those of the heroine of that tearful ballad. "My only regret is that we cannot suit ourselves with an estate. The M'Killop country has passed entirely into the hands of an English Duke" (the probabilities are that his Grace did not find it a very heavy handful), "and there is no other appropriate settlement open at present. Cairnarvoch is a sadly dull place—the neighbours distant, and not to our mind; and so this plan of taking in our shooting tenants does not seem amiss. I am sure we shall get on very happily together. M'Killop has reserve, but he is quite the jontleman. My daughter is as you see her—too brusk—too outspoken. I wish she could take a little of the polish of her stepsister, keeping her own heart, which is a kind one, although she does her best to conceal it. But you will make allowances for her; it is all the wild M'Whannel blood, which is not tamed in a day, as I daresay *you* know, Mr Cameron." Thus appealed to, Bertrand gave a knowing look, intended to signify that any one who attempted to tackle a M'Whannel, would, in his opinion, find tough work cut out for him; and Morna, jumping up, cried out, " Mamma, if you give such a dreadful account of me, these poor gentlemen will be afraid to drive home with us in the dark; and if we stay here much longer, it will be dark before we get home. Do order the carriages."

The order was given, and two large uncovered omnibuses were speedily at the door. In the foremost the ladies and gentlemen and the lighter baggage were bestowed; and the other being loaded with the servants, dogs, and heavier *impedimenta*, a start was effected.

It will not do to indicate their exact route. The Celtic imagination is highly pitched, and the temper of the race sometimes a little stiff; and if we were to particularise, who can say what might come of it? Who can say how many Mornas, and M'Killops, and M'Kechnies, not to mention untamable M'Whannels, might swoop upon us, terrible as the army of "the Phairshon," and strident as the overwhelming music of that celebrated host? Far from us be any such indiscretion. We may safely say, however, that the route was a beautiful one, though the road was hilly, and its engineering reflected more credit on the æsthetic, than on the practical, turn of its contriver.

The sun had just set behind the distant hills of Mull, but the sky was without a cloud, and glorious with that warm and mellow tint which comes not often on the northern sky, but coming casts on it a beauty unknown to the heavens of the South, where Night usurps with indecent haste the kingdom of the Sun, allowing no brief courtesy of twilight. Yet not to twilight does this mellow tint belong, but to a certain benign middle light between it and the sun's departure. Lacking the glory of the sun, yet lacking the mystery of the dusk, it withholds the ruder revelations of the one and the weird transformations of the other. Seen by it, every object retains its identity, but with each harsher detail refined and softened. Seen by it, the purple hills, though their outlines are severe as against a moonlit sky, may indeed be said to bloom; and the wild cataract, leaping in its glory, to cast itself down in softlier falling sheets of silvery tissue from the height; and the thousand variations of the forest foliage to blend into the one excellence of an ideal verdure; and the sunset breeze rippling the bosoms of quiet mountain-tarns, to lay on them a chastened lustre—the pathetic impress, as it were, of the sun's pure "good-night." "The stars of earth," as Schiller calls the flowers, may pensively veil somewhat of their brightness—a fitting tribute to him who is away, their glory and their life; yet from them, in their sweet eclipse, a compensating fragrance rises, and fresher than the incense offered to their present lord are the odorous sighs they breathe when he is gone— waiting for the sympathetic light of their sister stars above.

It was a delicious evening, and its soft influence, and the great beauty all around, and the stillness—the sudden hush which falls upon the world when the sun disappears, as if Nature paused a moment and muttered the breathless question—"Will he return?"—all the deep influences of the hour and scene might well make speech a profanation, and silence praise; and silence fell upon the party.

It must be admitted that Pigott's taciturnity was probably due to a constitutional bias in that direction, and Mrs M'Killop's, without doubt, to the more sublunary influence of an after-dinner sleep. But Bertrand was in a seventh heaven. Nature and Beauty were revealing themselves to him in their most benignant aspects, touching his heart with the fire of a hundred enthusiasms, and stirring all the romance and poetry of his soul into a sort of rapturous life.

Looking over the splendid hills, his spirit swelled with a patriotic joy, and he thought, "At last! Scotland! *my* country!" Here he was living and moving amid scenes that hitherto had been but the shadowy accessories of a thousand day-dreams. On these very hills, the mighty king of Morven had mustered his hosts to go forth to the battle with Lochlin; in these hollow glens they had gathered to the joyous "feast of shells;" across these shimmering waters they had sped their dark prows, burning to reap harvests of death with biting brands that "never gave a second wound"—Fingal, Ossian, and Oscar, and Gaul, the peerless son of Morni! The wild strains of ecstatic minstrels, the clash of armour, the battle-cry, the wailing dirge, seemed to live in his ears; the sheen of beamy spears, the waving of banners, the streaming locks of heroes rushing to the maelström of the fray, rose to his mental vision. The clear sky-line of the mountains seemed thronged with shadowy hosts, and, on the margin of the sea, stood the fair forms of other years—Bragela, and Evirallin, and white-armed Strina-Dona. And who were these that came like the mists, hovering, slow——

"What a delicious curd there was on that salmon at dinner!" here broke in the rasping voice of Mrs M'Killop; and though the remark (no doubt from the depths of slumber) was not followed by another, but tapered off into a succession of snores, snorts, gasps, and wheezes, it acted as "a word of power." The shadowy hosts halted in their rush, when the salmon rose in its material curdiness; at the sound of the earthy artillery which followed, they fled quaking back to Valhalla; and Bertrand, tumbling headlong out of cloudland, shocked against the cold earth, as the eagle falls pierced by the bullet of prosaic man.

He glanced rapidly round at his companions, as if half fearing that they might be conscious of his fanciful excursion, and half indignant at his rude recall. Mrs M'Killop's eyes were closed, her head moved in a suave rhythm with the sound of her snoring; she was beyond suspicion and the reach of wrath, and a well-pleased smile on her full lips suggested that her late repast was being re-enacted in a succulent dream.

Pigott, cold and wooden, was fixedly staring at the rug upon his knees; but Bertrand found that Morna was curiously looking at him.

"I—I was admiring that mountain," he said, in an apologetic tone; "what is its name?"

"That is Ben Scarrig," replied Morna.

"It is magnificent."

"Yes, it is a very fine hill."

"And how beautifully clear the outline is!"

"Yes, but I prefer it with some mist. It is wonderful sometimes to see the mist marching up from the sea, stealing through these woods below, and creeping along the ridges, just as if it had started to reach the top, like something living—with a purpose."

"Like an army of phantom sea-kings storming the height," cried Bertrand, suspecting a congenial spirit.

"It moves too gently for that," said Morna; "more like a procession of phantom pilgrims visiting the cairn of some great soldier who had died a hermit and a saint, and been buried in his cell far away up there on the top of the mountain."

"Miss Grant, you are quite a poetess."

"No, no, I was only following your idea—only an imitator; it is the story of Columbus's egg."

"I wonder what Pigott's simile would be?" said Bertrand; "what is it like, Pigott?"

"Which? the egg, or the hermit, or the mountain, or what?"

"The mist."

"Produce the mist, and I may be able to tell you."

"There wouldn't be half the imagination, you wouldn't have half the credit, Captain Pigott, if you saw it before your eyes."

"Oh, I'm a prose author; but, if it must be a procession of some sort; I should say a string of phantom tourists, headed by the adventurous Cook."

"Doesn't he deserve to be among them, Miss Grant?"

"Yes, I don't really think he is half ethereal enough for our society."

"You should let me sleep, then, if I am not to be among the prophets; or, better still, will you let me smoke, Miss Grant?"

"Of course, pray do."

"Then I will, and listen dreamily to your sweet discourse."

"Oh, but we shall be too shy to say anything worth listening to, when we know that you are sneering at us all the time."

"Bertrand is too conceited to be silenced by anything," said Pigott.

"But perhaps I am not."

"Smokers never sneer."

"I won't trust you; you had better go to sleep."

"Until Mrs M'Killop awakes, I must watch over my young friend."

"Why, what *can* you mean?"

"I mean that, after Mrs M'Killop's formidable account of your ancestors, whose fierce disposition you are said to inherit, I couldn't conscientiously close an eye upon the lad's safety. I once read a ballad—perhaps you know it—'Glenfinlas' by name. I have a shocking memory, but I think it tells how a gallant sportsman, Lord Ronald, went out to hunt the dun deer, and in his forest-hut was visited by just such a young lady as yourself, who, however, presently turned into a colossal lady-fiend, and made a light supper of the unhappy young nobleman."

"Pray, smoke, Captain Pigott."

"But listen. Your ancestors, the Mac-Wanels——"

"*MacHoo-annel! MacHoo-annel!*" cried Mrs M'Killop, waking up, and shouting the words like a slogan.

"The application I reserve to a future diet, as your ministers say," remarked Pigott. "Yes, Mrs M'Killop, I admit that my pronunciation is feeble: it is one of the many failings of the Saxon."

"They are a miserable race," said Mrs M'Killop, relapsing at once into slumber.

"Instead of listening to Pigott's nonsense," said Bertrand, "suppose you sing us a song, Miss Grant?"

"But suppose I can't sing?"

"I know you can."

"How?"

"By the sound of your voice."

"That is *very* flattering. Well, I will admit that I do sing sometimes."

"Gaelic songs?"

"Sometimes."

"Will you, now?"

"I am afraid Captain Pigott would laugh, and if he did I should be angry, because I love these songs; I *like* my other songs, but I *love* the Gaelic."

"Pigott is a heathen and a Saxon, but he won't laugh at anything you sing; I'll answer for him."

"Even if he were ill-bred enough to think of such a thing," said Pigott, "fear would deter him; the blood of your untamed ancestors——"

"Now, Captain Pigott, I'm not going to be teased about my ancestors; they are mamma's hobby, not mine—pray let them rest in peace."

"Amen! but do sing a verse or two of a pibroch or a coronach——"

"You are laughing at me already, and that settles the matter. Mr Cameron, I will sing *you* a Gaelic song some other time when Captain Pigott is out of the way. I won't profane my *repertoire* by singing one to him."

"I belong to an oppressed nationality, and I kiss the rod," said Pigott; "but at least you will let us have a song in the vulgar tongue?"

"You don't deserve it, but I will be generous. You must light your cigar first, though; I'm sure it will make you more civil."

"Thus coerced, I yield," said Pigott, lighting up; and Morna sang.

Bertrand had rightly surmised—she *could* sing. Moreover, she chose a song to which her voice was exactly suited, one of the sweetest of those Lowland melodies which the genius of the country and the sympathy of the heart can teach a true, pure, Scottish voice to sing to a perfection seldom reached by any alien with all the advantages of artistic culture. Morna's voice was very true and pure, and with frequent tones of genuine pathos in its large compass.

> " I see her in the dewy flowers,
>   I see her sweet and fair;
> I hear her in the tunefu' birds,
>   I hear her charm the air.

> There's not a bonnie flower that springs
>   By fountain, shaw, or green—
> There's not a bonnie bird that sings,
>   But minds me o' my Jean.
>
> O blaw, ye westlin winds, blaw saft,
>   Amang the leafy trees,
> Wi' balmy gale, frae hill and dale,
>   Bring hame the laden bees;
> And bring the lassie back to me,
>   Wi' her twa glancin' een;
> Ae blink o' her wad banish care,
>   Sae lovely is my Jean."

The air and the words, and the voice that sang them, seemed all to be the natural outcome of the scenery and the hour; and Bertrand felt that, if then and there the voice of singing was to be heard, that was the voice and that the song he would have chosen. There were the dewy flowers she sang of—the blue-bell and the fox-glove, the wild-rose and the heather—and there the tinkling chime of mountain springs—and the hills, and the dales, and the pensive light, and the darkening shaws, and the plaintive murmur of the night-breeze stealing across the moorlands, balmy with the breath of pine and gorse, and all manner of delightful thymy fragrance. It seemed to Bertrand that Morna's fresh voice set to music all these gracious surroundings, and infused their spirit into the tender passion of her "woodnotes wild."

"Beautiful! Miss Grant—perfectly beautiful!" he cried, with enthusiasm; "a thousand thanks."

"Such a voice," said Pigott, "might even sing the songs of the Ojibbaway, and achieve a triumph."

"*Even* sing them, Captain Pigott?" gobbled Mrs M'Killop, who was again awake; "indeed! if my girl is not competent to sing *them*, or anything else, I don't know who should be, after all the Signors and the Herrs that have been drilling at her."

"I don't think my masters would quite take that as a compliment, mamma," laughed Morna; "but the less I say about them the better. And now, Mr Cameron, it is my turn to ask for a song."

"If I begin to think how badly my performance will sound after yours, I shall get nervous; so I won't think, but sing without a preface."

And so Bertrand contributed his mite to the concert, singing in a pleasant, capable baritone, one of the English ballads of the day, which

Mrs M'Killop pronounced to be "mawkish," although the singer's voice seemed to her to have promise. Then Pigott was called upon, but laughed the notion to scorn, and named the driver as his substitute, who declined the office; but, being peremptorily ordered by Mrs M'Killop to perform on the instant and in Gaelic, eventually did so, and at great length, letting loose a flood of low, dolorous, guttural sounds, which seemed always on the point of dying out, but were perpetually rallied back to life by a sort of hiccupy cry of "hinyo."

"Did he die?" asked Pigott, when the man came at last to a close.

"Die? who?" said Mrs M'Killop.

"The gentleman in the ballad," said Pigott.

"There was nothing about death or a gentleman in the man's song; it was quite a funny little tale of love, and about a cow, and a shepherd, and three crows—full of wit and merriment."

"But some one groaned in the chorus, surely?"

"No, no; that was an exclamation of joyful surprise."

"It must be a wonderfully expressive language."

"It is indeed; we'll make him sing another."

"Oh, Mrs M'Killop, that would be taxing the poor fellow too much; and, by the by, we are not going to let *you* off. We must insist—and indeed, it is my call—upon a song from you."

Pigott found he had got from the frying-pan into the fire. His request was instantly complied with, and Mrs M'Killop, in a high, reedy voice, full of cracks and fissures, plunged straight into an intricate ballad, in which some Scottish maid tested her true love, as Rosalind did in the forest of Arden. It involved a series of lengthy dialogues between the lover and his disguised mistress, which Mrs M'Killop gave with great dramatic spirit, gruffening her voice for the male part, and reducing it to a sort of asthmatic whistle for the arch utterances of the fair beguiler.

"Yes, it is full of pathos," she remarked, in accepting the applause which followed; "and it is said to be founded on an event in the life of my great-grandmother, Mrs M'Kechnie of Tillywheesle—in Prince Charlie's time."

"Did the Prince play Orlando on the occasion?"

"Fie! Captain Pigott, fie! fie! fie! The M'Kechnie was the lover, of course; although there *is* a naughty idea in Scotland, such as you hint at. She was beautiful, you see—(indeed, it belongs to the race to be beautiful)—and the Prince, dancing with her at Holyrood, is said to have made a point of it, that from that hour she should be called 'The White Rose of Tillywheesle'—but that was all. And now I must give you a song about dear Prince Charlie;" and she did—several, in fact, and kept pretty steadily "in possession of the floor" for the rest of the journey, only suffering one song by Morna and one by Bertrand to be edged in between her performances, which she accompanied by stiffish notes of explanation, and not a few strange genealogies.

It was with much satisfaction, therefore, that the rest of the party found themselves at last entering the avenue.

The twilight had deepened, for it was past eleven o'clock, but still our travellers had light enough to see that the place was one of great beauty. The house was large, old, and irregular. Probably it had originally been in the old Scottish style; but a succession of additions had developed it into a very picturesque nondescript, the general result of which was a square battlemented tower, rising in state among tall gables with their "corby-stairs," supported on either flank by wings of a lower and lighter class of building, ornamented with a profusion of turrets and pinnacles. The situation of the house was very striking. It stood on a broadish plateau, which sloped away to the front in gentle declivities and undulations, but descended at the back of the house in a sheer rocky precipice, the base of which was lashed by the tumultuous waters of a cascade, roaring down a steep glen which here expanded into a valley, the waters widening themselves into a river, and winding round one flank of the plateau so as to run for half a mile parallel with, but far below, the avenue. In front of the house, beyond an acre or two of lawn, there was no attempt at a park. The natural wood had been cut out, indeed, in divers places, so as to give expanse and variety, and, here and there, to uncover the full proportions of some giant of the forest; but underneath, the heather and the bracken had it all their own way,—at least they did their best to dispute supremacy with those unsightly boulders and protruding rocks which bring grief to the hearts of reclaiming landowners. At the distance of a mile from the front of the house, the ground rose again into hills, backed in the distance by veritable mountains. Behind the house, the glen divided the lowest spur of another range, and, on the left flank, a narrow cultivated valley, already whitening to the harvest, ran for half a mile or so, when it was hemmed in and stopped by formidable banks of boulder, the outposts of the mountains that rose behind. Mountains, mountains everywhere.

"Glorious!" exclaimed Bertrand.

"What a trap for black game!" muttered Pigott, indicating the bright little bit of corn-land.

"I hope to goodness they haven't forgot supper," suggested Mrs M'Killop.

"They're awake, at all events," said Morna, as with a mighty clangour the great iron-studded doors were thrown open, letting loose some half-a-dozen terriers, who barked and pranced and ramped on the steps, as if prepared to do battle against all comers.

"Down, Bodach! For shame, Frioch! Bob,

you little viper!" exclaimed Morna, jumping lightly from the carriage, and plunging in among the canine rabble, who forthwith changed their wrathful clamour into yells and screams of affection and delight. "Down, dogs all!"

"The noise of the dogs," said Mrs M'Killop, as she slowly descended, "is a little trying; but the effect is baronial and commy faw, so I encourage it. None of them bite except Wasp, which is a mercy. Is supper ready, Jinkyson?"

"Supper is ready, ma'am," said an austere-looking butler, who, with two liveried satellites, had appeared at the entrance.

"Let us go in, then, gentlemen; you are welcome to Cairnarvoch." And with a gracious flourish she waved them into the hall, all the dogs strenuously flattening their baronial noses against Bertrand's calves, which, however, remained unbitten, the truculent Wasp being probably off duty for the evening.

CHAPTER III.

UNDER Mrs M'Killop's guidance, Bertrand and Pigott traversed an ancient and lofty octagonal hall, its far-away ceiling lost in mysterious shadows, which the lights below could not dispel, and its dark pannelled walls displaying, every here and there, some memorial of the olden time. Relics of the olden time, in such a mansion, and in such a district, are synonymous with relics of war or the chase; and here they were in abundance—claymore, pistol, dirk, pike, targe, and gun, royal antlered heads and outspread wings; and, amid numberless other native *exuviæ*, some of a more perilous sport from Eastern jungles and the primeval Western forests. Bertrand, struck with the *coup d'œil*, paused involuntarily for inspection; but Mrs M'Killop was far too hungry to play cicerone, and, briefly introducing the apartment as "the Armoury," preceded them into a room on the other side of the hall; and here they found their host. Like may draw to like in other matters, but it is almost a truism to say that by the law of contrast, rather than of similarity, people appear to guide themselves in their matrimonial selections. So much so, that if a matron of extra volume and self-assertion enters a drawing-room, we are disappointed if her announced husband does not prove to be a meek and shambling *homunculus;* and in like manner, from a husband's bigness of bone, voice, manner, and general amplitude, do we not reason down directly to a crumpled and depressed little wife at home?

If Mrs M'Killop had been entirely subject to this general law, her husband should have combined the stature of Tom Thumb with the humility of Uriah Heep; but, though he was as unlike her as possible, the principle of contrast was not thoroughly carried out, for Mr M'Killop was ordinary-looking and well-sized, and had no special abasement of manner, though his manner was unobtrusive, and his voice was quiet. He was elderly, almost old; his square, massive head, thatched with a close-growing crop of white hair; his features decidedly coarse and heavy, but his grey eyes were very keen and full of intelligence. If he had given his eyes anything like fair-play, no one could have said that he was a stolid-looking man; but he had a trick of averting them and casting them down—particularly in conversation—and thus, his light being hid under a bushel, people missed it, and did say that he looked like an owl.

His manner was formal and his speech was slow, suggesting caution, however, rather than pompousness; and his accent did not, as his wife's did, at once betray his nationality.

"Here we are, M'Killop!" cried that lady, bouncing into the room; "Captain Pigott and Mr Cameron, this is my husband;" and she pointed towards him with one finger, as who should say, "an appanage of our own royal state."

"I am glad to see you back again, Elizabeth," said her husband, quietly; "and" (shaking hands cordially with the strangers) "you are very welcome to Cairnarvoch, gentlemen: you have come a long way for sport, and I hope we shall find plenty of it for you. Where did you join parties?"

"We rongdavood at Ardrishaig; we had a little refreshment at Carrimorag; we have driven twenty-five miles since; and we're all starving. Now, that's all we're going to tell you till you give us supper. Jinkyson says it is ready, so come along; there's a flimsiness about all hotel diet, and I protest I feel as if I had tasted neither black nor white since morning;" with which remark, so creditable to her digestive organs, she led the way into the dining-room.

The supper was undeniably good; too good, seemingly, to admit of any rival subject in Mrs M'Killop's thoughts, as, with a fixed eye, and a velocity approaching voraciousness, she ministered to her obstreperous appetite, with never a word or a look to cast at those around her. Her husband, though he ate nothing, was equally silent; so was Morna; and as Pigott and Bertrand were both tired and hungry, they felt no call to make conversation; so the meal was almost a silent one for a considerable time. Pace, however, and concentration, will tell. By degrees, the half-satisfied, half-wistful look of the after-dinner vulture stole over Mrs M'Killop's face; she laid down her knife and fork definitively at last, and then there was no longer silence, we may be pretty sure.

"Well?" she commenced, looking at her husband, who, however, made no response. "Well?" she reiterated, in a sharper key; whereupon her husband looked up, and said "Well?" too.

"You eat nothing, and yet you say nothing," went on his wife; "one would think you might try to be a little more sociable."

"To tell you the truth, nothing occurred to me that seemed likely to be of interest to you, Elizabeth."

"Well, you might ask a question or two, at all events, if it was only to show your interest in us."

"Really, I don't think I have anything of moment to ask."

"That's flattering, that's complimentary," snapped his better half: "I've been away for a fortnight, and he has nothing particular to ask me!"

"Yes, by the by," amended M'Killop; "how is old Mr M'Dougal's gout?"

"Pshaw! Gout! That is not a subject for the table, M'Killop."

"It is often connected *with* the dinner-table, they say. Eh, gentlemen?"

"Is that a joke?" asked his wife.

"No, I'm not aware that it is; but I shall be glad if it amuses you," replied M'Killop, stolidly.

"There! that is exactly like you—yourself all over!"

It is notoriously seldom, in a complimentary sense, that a man is told by his wife that he reaches his own standard; and to allay symptoms of stormy weather, and stop the bickering of his hosts, Bertrand struck in and turned the subject. Glancing round the dark-wainscoted room, he remarked upon its venerable aspect, and asked if the pictures on the walls represented ancestors of the host or hostess.

"Oh dear, no!" replied the latter—"modern daubs belonging to the people of the house. Ours were all burned in the 'forty-five.'"

"Indeed!" said Pigott: "how unlucky! May I ask who burned them?"

"Who? why, bless the man! why, the enemy, of course."

"Oh, of course!" said Pigott, wondering, however, as so many others have wondered, what made that epoch so specially fatal to so many families, there being no historical record of burning and sacking. Who burned or carried off the pictures, mutilated the pedigrees, tore up the patents, and generally obliterated all evidence of age and dignity? It is almost as mysterious as Sir Bernard Burke's ingenuity in resuscitating, for families thus bereft, their historical prestige, or the providential care with which Wardour Street seems to have guarded so many of the authentic relics of their past.

"Yes," reiterated Mrs M'Killop, "burned in the 'forty-five.'"

"Your people were out in the 'forty-five,' I suppose, Mrs M'Killop?" inquired Bertrand.

"To a boy."

"And Mr M'Killop's also?"

"To tell you the truth," said the host, "I don't know; I never interested myself much in these subjects. I suspect, if they were out, they had no pictures to burn, or I should know more about them, perhaps."

"It seems so strange to me not to take an

interest in one's ancestors," said Bertrand, simply. "If mine had not been out in the 'forty-five,' I would have disowned them—I would have changed my name."

"Ah! yes; but there is most likely a difference between our cases; when a man has really had ancestors of position and distinction——"

"M'Killop is a very prosy man," interrupted his wife; "he thinks of nothing but the present generation. It is the way of this vile money-making age to laugh at the past."

"No, no," said M'Killop, "I don't. If I had had a grandfather——"

"No one would suppose you had, to hear you talk; one would say you had come off the parish."

"There is no good pretending——"

"Some people are so conceited they would go the length of denying their own 'forbears,' just that the world might say, 'How clever he is! He is a self-made man!'—all miserable vanity."

"I don't pretend to be cleverer than my neighbours, but I am, such as I am, a self-made man."

"Vanity, vanity!—all miserable vanity!"

"It is no discredit to my father——"

"Vanity! vanity! Say grace after meat, M'Killop."

The host complied, and by this devotional device his wife got rid of a topic which did not seem to be to her mind.

"You are a Scotchman, I presume, Mr Cameron, from your name and your allusions?" said Mr M'Killop.

"Yes, I am," replied Bertrand.

"Yes," burst in Mrs M'Killop; "and if you would ever give one a chance of getting in a word, instead of for ever spouting your Radicalism, I would have told you that Mr Cameron ought to be *particularly* welcome here."

"I am sure, Elizabeth, he *is* particularly welcome. I hope he is quite satisfied of that."

"Blood is thicker than water, M'Killop; Mr Cameron is a kinsman."

"Indeed!"

"Yes, distant indeed, but countable, where there is no objection on either side; and I am sure I have none," with a suave bow of interrogation to Bertrand.

He, however, had thought this kinsmanship all very well for once, as a joke, but did not relish its becoming accepted as a fact in sober earnest. So his reply was a very slight, very stiff inclination, stiffened, no doubt, by a sly glance which Pigott shot across the table at him.

"But there is another reason," continued Mrs M'Killop, "why he ought to be especially welcome here; and that is, that he is a neighbour."

"I don't quite understand that," replied her husband.

"Oh! Mrs M'Killop," said Bertrand, "you state my claim too strongly, as I am only the kinsman of a neighbour; if, indeed, Aberlorna is near this."

"Oh yes, it is; M'Killop, he is a Cameron of Aberlorna."

"A Cameron of Aberlorna!" exclaimed the host, in a tone of unaccountable astonishment, his eyes opening wide upon Bertrand, and his whole manner and expression galvanised, as it were, by some sudden and even painful interest. "A Cameron of Aberlorna," he repeated, after a pause; and then, as if mechanically— "how?"

"Why, simply enough," replied Bertrand; "I am Sir Roland Cameron's nephew—the son of his elder brother."

"Sir Roland Cameron's nephew — the nephew of Sir Roland Cameron!" repeated M'Killop, as if by transposing the sentence to familiarise himself with a difficult idea, and keeping his fixed gaze steadily on the young man.

"Yes, his nephew," repeated Bertrand, with a puzzled look. "Is he a friend of yours?"

"And the son of his elder brother?" continued the host, disregarding the question.

"Yes; it seems to surprise you?"

"And how do you come to be here?" asked M'Killop, in an absent voice, but with the same intense look in his face.

"Pardon me," said Bertrand, "I scarcely understand."

"M'Killop!" cried his wife, "what has come over you? What are you staring at? Where are your manners? How does Mr Cameron come to be here! a nice question to ask! You'd better go to bed at once; you seem to be talking in your sleep."

Hereupon Mr M'Killop seemed, with an

effort, to retire into his usual manner, and said apologetically, dropping his eyes into their normal position, "I meant, of course, that with Sir Roland's shooting lying idle, it seemed curious that Mr Cameron should care to be a tenant here."

"Ah! you see, Mr M'Killop, my uncle doesn't take the same view; he has not offered me the shooting of Aberlorna."

"Did you not suggest it to him?"

"I would rather go without shooting for the rest of my life than ask a favour."

"That's carrying pride a long way; with an uncle too, and when the property will be your own, under Providence, some day," said M'Killop.

"I like it," cried the hostess; "it is the old spirit, the real old spirit."

"Do you think you always act on it, Elizabeth?" asked her husband.

"Tut! you *are* talking in your sleep, and I must set you the example of going to bed. Come away, Morna. Good-night, gentlemen; I hope you'll sleep sound after your journey. Make my husband show you your rooms at once; he's not fit company for the parish idiot

—staring and talking like a perfect gomeril. Good-night."

"My wife is a little hard upon me," said M'Killop, with a smile; "but perhaps her hint is a good one. I daresay you are ready for bed; but perhaps you would like to go to the smoking-room first?"

"Thanks," said Pigott; "I think we have done enough in that way already, eh, Bertrand?"

"Yes, I'm all for bed. By the by, Mr M'Killop, did you say you were intimately acquainted with my uncle?"

Again there was the same strange look in M'Killop's eyes as he lifted them to Bertrand's face, and replied,—

"No, I did not say so—no."

"You know him, of course? I thought you seemed interested about——"

"Only an old association—an old recollection that came across me—nothing more. I have no acquaintance with Sir Roland; I never saw him even. Now I'll show you your rooms."

So saying he conducted them by corkscrew stairs and winding passages to their destination, and left them with a hearty "goodnight."

Our two travellers were delighted with their quarters. The suite consisted of a sitting-room and two bedrooms opening off it on opposite sides. The sitting-room was a perfect *bijou*, circular in form, and high and roomy in its dimensions. The wainscoting was of black oak, the floor was of black oak, and the antique furniture was of the same material; but the sombre effect was relieved by the curtains and coverings, which were all of a brilliant tartan. A fine collection of roebucks' heads ornamented the walls, running round them, about a yard from the ceiling, in a circle only broken over each door by the substitution of a royal stag's head. For other decoration, there were one or two proof engravings of Landseer's masterpieces. A vase of fresh flowers was on the central table, and a lounging-chair on either side of the fireplace, in which an aromatic fire of peat and pine sparkled cheerily. Their bedrooms proved to be as neat and comfortable, and with the same picturesque quaintness in all the details.

"It is an undeniable billet," said Pigott, as,

emerging from their dormitories, each subsided into a seductive "fire-sider." "I pass the M'Killop establishment. I give it an A 1 register for three calendar months. There is no nonsense about the cook who turned out that supper to-night, mind you. As for the liquor, it struck me as strangely palatable, and there seems to be no tightness in that department. We shall not have to fall back upon whisky-toddy if the butler is half as gentlemanlike as he looks. He beats his master in that respect; but that is a mere matter of detail. This room is really a gem, and this chair. Thank goodness the beds are not feather-beds! Touch up the fire, Bertrand; what a jolly smell it has! We'll smoke in this room when it rains; or at nights, if the natives are a bore. Talking of them, did you ever see old Alec Reed the prize-fighter? No? —ah, I daresay he was dead before your time. Well, M'Killop is wonderfully like him; he has more teeth, and the full complement of eyes, but otherwise his very image. How the old fellow stared when he heard who you were! did you notice? and with such a queer, misty look in his eyes—softening of the brain evidently; but I believe they're never violent with that disease, so perhaps we have no great right to complain. As for his wife, an application of galvanism to a very large ill-finished "Aunt-Sally" would——; but, by the by, she is your relative, so let her pass with the rest."

"Not as my relative, please," cried Bertrand.

"I beg a thousand pardons; your 'countable connection.'"

"Countable connection! why, the woman must be crazy. It is the most confounded piece of impudence I ever heard of!"

"What! you disown the kinship?"

"I should rather think I do; and, what's more, I'll tell her so if she ever mentions it again."

"Ah! Bertrand, you're not half a Celt; you don't understand the patriarchal system,—how wide the family branches spread, how deep the roots strike, how closely they interlace ever so far away from the parent stem—when there is anything to be made by it, of course."

"One thing, however, I *do* know, and that

is, that I'm not going to allow this old harridan to interlace herself with me as a relation, root or branch. Don't speak of her; she's the only black spot in the business."

"Oh! you're pleased, then?"

"I am indeed: what a splendid country! what air! what hills! what a sky that was tonight! and what a jolly old place this is! It's like coming into a new world; I declare it is. Do you remember when we were driving through that gorge to-night where there was an old tower hanging over the waterfall?"

"Yes, I think so."

"Ah, Pigott! what did you feel then?"

"As far as I can remember, I felt that if Mrs M'Killop's head remained another minute on my shoulder, I *must* strike it with my clenched fist."

"Pshaw! you—really you *are* too abominably prosaic."

"All very well for you who were sitting beside a pretty little light-weight: if her head had dropped on to your shoulder by accident, it wouldn't have greatly signified; but to have a thing like a 64-pound shot wobbling about on your shoulder, gurgling and snorting like a grampus!—why, it would crush the poetry out of the Poet-Laureate himself. Do you know your countable—I mean Mrs M'Killop's head is really a thing quite by itself."

"Oh! bother Mrs M'Killop's head! What a charming song that was of Miss Grant's—the first one!"

"Yes, it was; and she is a very nice girl, I think."

"Very; her song will haunt me all night."

"I wish I could believe it would haunt me, but no such luck. I shall be haunted by something very different."

"What?"

"Oh! that poignant song of her mother's, where the steam-saw movement came out so strong in the high notes. Don't you remember it?"

"I scarcely heard her; her voice did not affect me more than the rumbling of the wheels or the creaking of the springs. The fact is, Miss Grant's song sent me off into a sort of reverie; I was in dreamland."

"Oh! you were?"

"Yes."

"And—and—well?"

"It seemed to me that in Miss Grant's song I heard the voice of the *genius loci*."

"Who is he?"

"Who?"

"The *genius loci*, of course."

"What an ass I am to talk to you about anything—about anything worth talking of."

"It's an indiscretion you don't often commit, I'll say that for you."

"Good-night, Pigott," cried Bertrand, jumping up. "I'm too satisfied with everything to let you get a rise out of me to-night, much as you would like it, I see. Good-night! sleep sound.

> "'I see her in the dewy flowers,
>   Sae lovely and sae fair;
> I hear her in the tunefu' birds,'" &c.;

and so he retired singing to his roost, well filled the measure of his heart's content.

"Now that's what they call a mercurial fellow, impulsive, expansive, et cetera," growled Pigott to himself. "He goes through as many emotions in an hour as I do in a month. Well, well, variety is charming, perhaps, but that sort of thing would kill me in no time. And now to bed, to bed. A glorious night!" (looking out of window); "what a grousey bit of hillside! and oh! what a trap for black-game! Confound that fellow Wilson, he *has* forgotten my slippers, I believe! what am I to do?" And so to bed the two friends, one with his head among the stars, the other with all the sympathies of his soul accompanying his feet as they grope about for the missing slippers.

CHAPTER IV.

"In the name of everything hideous, Wilson, what is that intolerable row?" cried Pigott, starting from a half-sleep as his servant entered his room next morning. "Has rinderpest broken out among all the cats of the clan, or has Mrs M'Killop caught bronchitis, or what is it? it has been going on for hours, I believe."

"It's them bagpipes, sir," said Wilson, with grim contempt. "That there piper was a toonin' of them for breakfast, as they say, just down below here; and Mr Cameron, he came up and took them, and he's been workin' at them for ten minutes; but the piper's got them again, I see, so maybe the noise won't be quite so bad, sir."

"And what o'clock does this mean?"

"Nine o'clock, sir."

"And how long will this noise last?"

"I can't say, sir; I *did* ask the piper, but all he would say was, 'Till she was finished.' I expect he'll go on for a good bit, though. I don't think he's quite all there, sir."

"No more sleep for me, then; I'll get up. Mr Cameron is up, you say?"

"Oh yes, sir; up and out and about, hours ago."

"What a maniac!" growled Pigott, regretfully unearthing himself.

Bertrand had awakened early, fresh from slumbers sound and roseate dreams, and the view of the purple hills blooming in the morning sun that burst on him through his open window, had drawn him instantly from bed. Hastily dressing himself, he had sallied forth towel in hand, and following the river up to where a minor section of the cascade fell quietly into a clear pebbly basin, there enjoyed a bath worthy of the gods, curtained in with drooping boughs and foliage of the weeping birch, and with a carpet to step out on bright with a myriad "wildings of the wood." Returning to the house, he had fallen in with the piper, and instantly struck up the alliance with results so fatal to his friend's repose.

"There is one advantage about these abominable pipes," soliloquised Pigott as he descended to the breakfast-room musing upon the hidden uses of things, "that they *must* insure punctuality at breakfast. I don't believe the seven sleepers of Ephesus, or Rip Van Winkle, or any historical sleeper, would have been proof against that fellow's din. Ah, Bertrand! here you are! good morning! I thought you were out."

"Out! so I have been: such a morning! how could you lie in bed? I've just been putting myself to rights after my bath—a bath in a natural bath-room, all among the woods and rocks—a bath-room for an oread or a dryad; and since then I have been fraternising with that glorious fellow outside."

"What did you call him?"

"A glorious fellow—so he is—with such a jolly name, Hamish M'Erracher! I'm enrolled as his pupil, and begin the day after to-morrow."

"And pray where are the lessons to come off?"

"Oh, all about the place; on the terraces likely; one has to learn to march with them, you see."

"In that case," said Pigott, "I'll tell Wilson to have my things packed the day after to-morrow; 'the glorious fellow' has already given me a compound fracture of the right tympanum, and I'd be sorry to discover practically the effect of a duet between you and him. So off I go unless your education is to be carried on on the top of some fairly distant mountain."

"Oh, nonsense! better join the class. We mustn't let Hamish know you're a Sassenach, though; he mightn't like it; I suspect he might mutiny."

"I sincerely wish he would, and desert into the bargain. Here we are at the bottom of the corkscrew; where's the dining-room? Scotch breakfasts are never bad, that's one comfort—even Dr Johnson admits it; but this will require to be something extra to atone for the infernal prelude. Where on earth is the door?"

"Here, under the star of claymores; but stop, stop, Pigott, you mustn't go in without seeing Fin Ericsen's enchanted spear. Hamish says it worked a miracle once. It's a capital yarn. I'll tell it you. You must know that a certain Jarl Ergill—a sea-king, I suppose—cruising about among the isles, landed once upon a time at Skye——"

"And I don't think the Jarl will take much harm if we leave him there till after breakfast," said Pigott, coolly dismissing the legend and entering the breakfast-room.

The family party were already assembled; M'Killop poring over the papers; Morna fresh and bright, the very incarnation of health and good-humour; and Mrs M'Killop, with her tawdry splendour somewhat toned down, but still very gorgeous. "Wonderful punctuality!" she exclaimed as the two young men entered; "and I hope it means that you both slept well?"

"Thanks; I never slept sounder in my life," said Bertrand, "the proof of which is that I was up and out, three hours ago. The Spirit of the glens looked in at my window and called me."

"My sleep was also of the soundest," said Pigott, "the proof of which is that it would have lasted for three hours to come, but the Demon of the Storm shrieked in at my window and called me."

"Storm?" said Mrs M'Killop; "there was no storm."

"I speak of a dream, as I presume my friend does."

"Oh, do tell us about it, Captain Pigott; I delight in wonderful dreams," cried Morna.

"I dreamt, then, that a mighty wind came rushing out of—out of some place or another —straight at me where I lay, and I saw, carried on its awful wings, what seemed at first a jet-black cloud. Anon (mark the word), as it drew nearer, it put on the guise of a gigantic kettle of sinister aspect—steam coming out of its spout with horrible sibilations, and I seemed to say to myself, 'Lo! the Demon of the Storm!' but it drew nearer and nearer, and now it was a swarm of bees clustered together in a mass bigger than many hay-stacks, and it made a booming, whizzing, shrieking, snarling sound, altogether indescribable, yet very alarming, and then I felt positive it *was* the Demon of the Storm, but was too frightened to say so, and tried to put my head under the blankets. But it was too late; the swarm was down upon me—it overwhelmed me. I received a frightful sting in the right ear, and woke up with a cry of agony to find my servant quietly telling me that it was nearly breakfast-time—because the bagpipes were playing."

"Oh, an allegory!" cried Morna; "a most poetical way of snubbing poor Hamish, and very ungrateful of you, too, because he was performing his very choicest *morceaux* in your honour. I heard him; he gave us twice as much as usual. He always likes to make an impression upon new-comers."

"It is very good of him," said Pigott; "he achieved a complete success this morning."

"Poor Hamish will be in raptures," said Mrs M'Killop, who was rather mystified by the allegory.

"Apropos of spirits and demons, I hope you were not troubled by the ghost, Captain Pigott?" said Morna.

"I'm sorry to say I wasn't, Miss Grant; I'm getting very impatient to see one."

"Ah! you don't know Scotland."

"Indeed I do; and I've lived in many a house supposed to possess such a treasure, and yet always passed serene and ghostless nights."

"Perhaps you are not spiritual enough. A spirit-seer, they say, must be spiritual, magnetic, sympathetic, and all sorts of things,—which I am afraid you are not."

"Quite right, Miss Grant; he isn't," said Bertrand. "Pigott would never have seen the Holy Grail, for instance."

"Having a decided objection to heavy suppers, I don't think I could have qualified. They gormandised horribly at the Round Table, and the Holy Grail was an obvious result."

"There, Miss Grant, that shows you what he is."

"It is a shocking case of depravity," said Morna, "and I fear he is irreclaimable; but I am glad to see you are properly scandalised."

"Oh, I am perfectly orthodox—the Highland creed is my creed,—ghost, wraith, vision, water-kelpie,—I believe in them all; but have you really got a ghost here?"

"Oh yes, really and truly. Hamish saw him one night standing outside the square tower, all in white, drinking out of a long tumbler; and he heard him whistle, and then give a kind of sob or yawn; and then he stretched out his arms and disappeared in at the trapdoor in a puff of smoke, right into a room which an English gentleman was occupying, who never saw him—which shows you that everybody can't see ghosts, Captain Pigott; and then Mary saw him, and Peter, and——"

"My dear Morna," said her mother, "how can you be so absurd? No modern family like the proprietors of this house are entitled to have a ghost."

"The ghost might belong to the previous set," objected Pigott.

"Certainly not; no ghost of family would stay among *parvenus*."

"But still, knowing you were here, he might have ventured back, just for a flying visit. You see I am trying to make the best case for your spiritual friend, Miss Grant."

"I'm afraid we're all talking terrible nonsense," said Morna.

"Well, Morna, my dear, I think that's not to be denied. You and your mother are both first-rate hands at it," said M'Killop, looking up from the newspaper.

"Any news this morning, Mr M'Killop?" asked Pigott.

"Well, there appears to be a great awakening in the Australian preserved-meat trade, and that is great news for people colonially interested."

" I suppose so."

" Yes, for the successful establishment of that trade must have a prodigious effect on more than one colony. In fact, if this report is true, we are very near a crisis."

" A commercial crisis in more than one colony?"

" Clearly so," said M'Killop, warming with his theme—" clearly so; just tell me, in the first place, how would wool be permanently affected? that's a cardinal point; and, in the second place, what will be the effect of the first blush of the matter on that sensitive market? And, in the third place, as to tallow; that's another cardinal point; and——"

"In the fourth place, Mr M'Killop," cried his wife, "if that's your notion of sensible conversation, commend me to our nonsense. Wool, forsooth! and tallow! outrageous! these are nice subjects for a lady's breakfast-table."

It is a woeful thing for a man with one subject to have it summarily snubbed, and poor M'Killop was evidently in this predicament. He bore it meekly, however, and let the conversation flow on uninterrupted till it gravitated inevitably to his wife's one subject —her fatal pedigree—and then he interfered. If his speciality was distasteful to her, hers was evidently a red rag to him; so he rose and rescued his guests.

"I think," he said, "we'll be wasting too much of a fine morning, if we stay any longer in the house. Come away, gentlemen; and how would you like to kill the time to-day? for the 11th of August is always a weary day for young sportsmen."

"We must see the dogs first," said Pigott, "and by-and-by I would like to take a stretch on the hill, just to break in a bit for to-morrow; what say you, Bertrand?"

"Oh, I can't stand constitutional walking, and besides, I've rather set my affections on the river; I saw some splendid trout this morning."

"You must ask Morna to be your guide, then," said Mrs M'Killop; "she is our fisherman: she will show you the best pools, and do the honours of the river, and I'll come and see you fill your baskets."

"Will you really take charge of me, Miss Grant?" asked Bertrand.

"Oh yes, I will, if you'll promise to be obedient, to be quiet when I want you to be quiet, and to take the pools exactly as I wish. My discipline is very strict, for you see it is my only sport, and so I am in earnest about it."

"I will do my best to be docile, particularly as I am rather a poor hand at the sport."

"After luncheon, then?" said Morna.

"If you please."

"Come away, then, gentlemen, and we'll have a look at the kennels," said M'Killop, and the ladies were left alone.

"What a fine-looking young man he is!" murmured Mrs M'Killop, as the three gentlemen passed the window; "what a very fine-looking young man he is!" she repeated, addressing Morna.

"Which of them, mamma?"

"How can you ask? Mr Cameron, of course; the very picture of a chief."

"It is better than looking like a London shopkeeper, as you thought he did yesterday, mamma; but if he had seen as many chiefs as I have, I don't think he would thank you for the compliment."

"And why not, pray?"

"Because I suppose he is what people call good-looking, and the others, poor people, are not beautiful as a rule."

"Some people can see no good near home. Then Mr Cameron is so pleasant, and bright, and intelligent, and refined."

"He is certainly a gentleman—they both are—and pleasant, too, I think."

"It is a splendid property, too; ten thousand a-year at the least."

"His uncle's?"

"Yes, but it will be his."

"Only under Providence, as Mr M'Killop says."

"Don't be profane, Morna. There is a great deal to be done in a day's fishing."

"To-day I'm afraid not; the wind is not what I like: and just look at these white clouds—only look at them,—more coming up, too."

"Don't be perverse, child, and tease me."

"Tease! mamma!" exclaimed Morna, with much innocent astonishment.

"You know what I mean, you ungrateful monkey. I've arranged the opportunity for you, and you pretend not to see it."

"I was going to fish at any rate," said Morna, showing a very decided front to her mother; "and if you mean the opportunity of fishing with Mr Cameron, why, that will only spoil my sport; if you mean—if you mean anything else, he shan't go with me at all. Opportunity! What *do* you mean, mamma?"

"Oh, you silly, ridiculous girl! you take fun in earnest, and earnest in fun, always. I thought it would be a fine change for you to get a gentleman ghillie to manage your hooks and carry the basket, and be more amusing company than old Donald; but of course I'm misunderstood, and you fly out at your poor mother like—like—so unkind!"

"I'm sorry I misunderstood you, mamma," said Morna, and left the room.

"I wish that monkey Eila would stay away for a month!" soliloquised Mrs M'Killop; "*she* would never throw away a chance, and she'll be back again before—before any good can be done. This brat Morna with her high-mindedness is too aggravating."

The visit to the kennels pretty well consumed the interval between breakfast and luncheon—a somewhat inordinate time, it may seem; but, on the eve of such a festival as the 12th of August, a visit to the kennels is like the general inspection of an army, and the interview with the keepers as serious a business as a council of war on the eve of a general action. Considering all they had to do, and the method of doing it, the time was not unreasonable. M'Killop had a very good show of dogs; then dogs must have pedigrees, and pedigrees will have complicated strains; and dogs have performances always more or less barnacled with fiction; but complicated strains become more complicated when handled by a garrulous old keeper, and fiction breeds like a rabbit under the inspiration of a Celtic fancy. So that, to get through a score of dogs—to learn how this terrier, in a perfectly Homeric combat, with a hundred episodes, had slain an otter—and how that retriever had retrieved "a cawf" from a flood, and was then and there "able and willint to retrieve a ailiphant," with other similar histories,—was by no means the work of a moment. The keeper, indeed, could have spent much more time over it, although he monopolised almost every instant, and shouldered out of sight, twenty times at least, an anecdote of Mr M'Killop's, which was perpetually hovering on the edge of the conversation, about a certain bleary old setter named "Smut;" so that Smut's exploits remained in the obscurity which envelops those of "old Grouse in the gun-room." Mr Campbell, the keeper, it must be explained, was the retainer of the absentee proprietor of Cairnarvoch, and felt it incumbent upon him to contemn, snub, and generally sit upon, Mr M'Killop in his quality of *locum tenens* and interloper. Most of us have had a taste of the flagrant tyranny of old-servantism, either in our own establishments or, reflectively, in those of our friends; but Mr Campbell's tyranny was something beyond common experience; he quite out-heroded Herod in this line. Having long ago mastered his master, who was a limp spendthrift, and having weighed Mr M'Killop in the balance and found him wanting as sportsman and as gentleman, he had from the commencement assumed a double-distilled tone of superiority and dictation; and his temporary master having succumbed without a struggle, their relations were entirely reversed, and Mr Campbell's despotism was as complete as it was severe. His feelings on the arrival of the two sub-tenants were of a mixed character. On the one hand there was prospective gain, but on the other there was the fear that they might introduce revolutionary ideas. There was also a certain increase of work; how much of an increase depended a good deal on the ground he could maintain with the new-comers; so to-day his manner was more domineering and impudent than usual—it was tentative; he was seeing how far he could go.

"You have a capital lot of dogs, Mr M'Killop," said Bertrand, when the inspection was completed.

"I'm no jist sae weel aff as I've seen me," instantly replied the keeper. "A year or twa back ye micht hae said sae, but I hinna the encouragement I ance had"

"I'm sure, Campbell, you have all you ask," said his master.

"Oo ay—it's no that, of coorse; but a body hasna the same speerit 'workin' wi' a stranger like, espaicially when ae dug's as gude as anither til him."

"Come, come, Campbell," said M'Killop, with a deprecating laugh, "you're a little too hard upon me; but, talking of that, I want to settle the dogs for to-morrow; I think I know the dogs for the 'Twelfth' at all events. The Doctor has just given me his orders not to shoot this season, so I won't take a gun; but there are two gentlemen coming, and I want to give them the best of the kennel; so I was thinking we had better say Juno for one, and Pet for another, and then Dandy and Rollo, of course."

"Juno! Pat! Dandy! Rowley!" exclaimed the keeper, *crescendo*—" Rowley " being the climax of impossible selections. "Naither the tane nor the tither, nor the tither, nor the tither to the back o' that, Mr M'Killop."

"And why not, Campbell?"

"Because ye're gaun to tak' Lomond, and Boz, and Flora, and Wee Peter."

"And why not the others?"

"Because they're no gauin oot till the day after — maybe no till the day after that," replied the old rascal, dogmatically, filling his pipe.

"I would have liked Juno for them, and

Rollo," said Mr M'Killop, meekly feeling his way to a compromise.

"Weel, ye see, they canna *hae* Juno and Rowley; it's a' planned and ready, and I've tell't ye afore there canna be twa folk to manage sic matters."

"Oh, of course you know best, Campbell," and M'Killop struck his colours.

"Where are our dogs, keeper?" said Bertrand, who felt that he would like to brain the miscreant.

"Weel, I dinna richtly ken."

"Have the goodness to find out."

"Here, Sandy!" (to an underling)—"whaur was thae Inglish beests pitten?"

"In the auld kennel," replied Sandy.

"Round by, here," said old Campbell, slowly leading the way, and puffing volumes of smoke in the faces of the gentlemen. "There!" he said, when the kennel was reached, and four or five couple of well-bred, work-like setters and pointers dashed themselves against the railings, slobbering and yelping and barking, as dogs delight to do. "There!" and there was a world of concentrated depreciation in the keeper's tone.

"They look fit enough," said Pigott.

"Nice-looking dogs," said M'Killop—"eh, Campbell?"

The keeper removed his pipe, spat sardonically, and slowly shook his head with a sickly smile, but said nothing.

"You don't seem to think much of them?" said Bertrand.

"Weel, sir, to be oanest wi' ye, I maun say that I'm no jist that unco taen up wi' them."

"I can assure you the dogs are all of the best breeds."

"Belike sir, belike; I'd be sweered to say the contrar, but ye see there's a gae wheen best breeds, and there's no jist exacklee the same *bestness* in them a'."

"I'll venture to say that any real judge would pronounce these dogs to be first-rate, at any rate."

"It's no for me to say that I ken better than a'body else aboot dugs, but I think I *micht* ken something. I've been warkin' amang them fifty year, ony way."

"Oh, Campbell has great experience," said M'Killop, trying to throw oil upon the wave, but retreating in the direction of the other kennel.

"Well, Campbell," said Bertrand, with a laugh, though in a towering passion, "you have your opinion, and I have mine, and I hope if I have fifty years' experience I shan't change mine as to what makes a good dog."

"There's a wheen pints aboot thae dugs, sir," persisted Campbell, "that's no to my likin' ava. There's a want o' shouther in ane (to my een ony way, sir), and a want o' gird in anither; and that yally ane's nigh aboot kannel lame, I doot; and if ye lift the feet o' twa or three mair, ye'll see, I'm muckle afeared, that they're no a'thegither fit to traivel oor hills—and then they'll be a' clean strange to the grouse?"

"No, no," said Pigott; "that they're not. Most of them have been two seasons worked in Yorkshire, and some of them in Scotland. Show them birds enough, Campbell, and I'll be bound they'll do their work. Wait till you see the bag I make over a brace of them to-morrow, and you'll change your opinion. You'll find the shoulders, and the girths, and the feet all right, never fear."

"I never had nae consate o' Yorkshire dugs mysel'; but it may be as ye say, sir: still and with a', there's a gae hantle sheep on thae hills; and when a dug's no acquent wi' the grouse, and no that weel broken, into the bargain, and——"

"Tut! tut! Campbell," interrupted Bertrand, "you're determined to find fault; but you can't make us believe all these dismal things about the dogs, so it's no good jawing about it. Tell our lad I shall want the big black dog and the black-and-tan for to-morrow —Jet and Tom."

"And tell him I shall take Nell and Fan," said Pigott: and they walked away, leaving Campbell sorely crest-fallen. He gazed after them for a few minutes in silence: there was no mistake whatever about the tone of the two gentlemen; he would have, as he himself expressed it, to "pu' in his harns;" so he shook his head, and, knocking the ashes out of his pipe, summed up as he turned away, —"But jist let me catch auld M'Killop at ony o' *his* deevil's pliskies; if the young cock craws, the auld ane disna larn, or my name's no Duncan Campbell."

"How Mr M'Killop can put up with that old savage, I can't understand; he ought to be sacked on the spot," said Bertrand, when they were out of ear-shot.

"He certainly is an old sweep," said Pigott.

"M'Killop *must* be an old cad to stand him."

"Yes; it must be confessed 'the gentleman of position' doesn't take a very high one in his own establishment."

"Doesn't his wife sit upon him too?"

"She *is* rather down on him at times; but I doubt, after all, if she's the master. With all his quietness, I've seen him give her a look now and then with that queer eye of his that seemed rather to shut her up."

"He doesn't seem to be much taken up with her pedigree?"

"Well, you know, he *is* rather old to enjoy works of fiction; but talking of his eye, he seems to take a singular interest in you; every now and then I noticed him look up from his paper at breakfast this morning, and favour you with a very close inspection. Did you observe?"

"No, I didn't."

"You needn't take it as a compliment, I'm certain of that; there was a very queer look in his eye, but it wasn't admiration; I'll be hanged if I know what it was. He looked at you in the same way last night when he heard who you were. You noticed it then?"

"Pooh! the man was sleepy."

"Yes; but he couldn't be sleepy at breakfast, so I suppose it *must* be softening of the brain."

"Hush! here he is."

"I was afraid," laughed M'Killop, who here joined them, "that you and old Campbell would come to blows. You mustn't be too hard upon him, though; his manner is rather abrupt, but he has many sterling qualities—a very old and valuable servant."

"Oh, I've no doubt we shall be excellent friends," said Pigott, "when we understand each other. I'm sorry to hear you're not going to shoot to-morrow."

"No; the Doctor has quite decided that; I have a little weakness of the heart, and he is strong against hill-walking. I never was much of a shot, though, so the disappointment is not very great; but it is an ill wind that blows nobody good, and it will give you all the larger range."

"I am sure we are both very sorry for the cause," said Bertrand.

"I've asked a couple of friends, however, to shoot here for a day or two, and, under the circumstances, I'm sure you won't think it a breach of contract. By the by, Mr Cameron, one of them will be interested to see you—Mr Tainsh—he is your uncle's factor for the Aberlorna estate."

"I shall be delighted to see him, I'm sure," said Bertrand.

"Tainsh is quite the man of the district," continued M'Killop; "a great favourite. He does business for half the county, and I'll be bound to say he gets more shooting and more good dinners than most of us."

"Are you really going to fish this afternoon, Bertrand?" inquired Pigott.

"Yes, of course—and you?"

"I'm going to constitutionalise. Holloa! there are the pipes again! Lunch already! as I live by bread and certain addenda."

CHAPTER V.

When luncheon was over, Pigott started for his constitutional; and Morna, equipped for fishing, soon after appeared in the drawing-room, where were her mother and Bertrand.

"Oh, mamma!" she exclaimed, "how lazy of you! Not begun to get ready yet! You're robbing us of half our day."

"Bless me! I had forgotten all about it," exclaimed Mrs M'Killop, jumping up with great energy; "how stupid of me, to be sure! What part of the river are you going to?"

"To the Blue Rock pool first," said Morna.

"Very well, pray go on without me; I won't promise to overtake you young walkers, but I'll be there to see the first trout caught; and now I'm off to dress."

If Morna had been a little older or less ingenuous, or if she had had more previous experience of her mother's powers as a strategist, she would have coupled that lady's hints of the morning with her obliviousness of her appointment, and perfectly understood that the "Blue Rock pool" was rather more likely to come to Mrs M'Killop than to receive a visit from that lady on that afternoon, in which case Bertrand would certainly have had to fish by himself; but Morna suspected nothing, and went forth in her innocence to a long unchaperoned afternoon. Avoiding the upper waters, where the trees that everywhere overhung the stream rendered wading indispensable, she led the way to a point in the river where it ran through the little tract of corn-land rapturously noted by Pigott the night before as "a trap for black-game."

The afternoon was intensely hot; there was not a cloud—black, white, or grey—in all the sky; the sun blazed relentlessly; the limpid heat-vapour quivered on the moorlands, and not a breath of wind stirred the surface of the stream, woefully shrunk by the summer drought. A most unfortunate day for the sport, it seemed, and Bertrand remarked it. Morna differed, however.

"My idea," she said, "is, that where there is no difficulty there is no skill required, and where there is no skill there is no sport. When everything exactly suits—water, clouds, wind—any one can fill a basket; but in a day like this it requires fine fishing—the finest—high art; so this is the sort of day I like. Here we are at mamma's rendezvous; you can begin here, and I will go a little lower down, and we can pass each other in turn."

"Isn't that rather an unsociable arrangement?" said Bertrand.

"There is no help for it, I'm afraid," replied Morna.

So Bertrand sat himself down and selected his flies, adjusted his rod, and began to whip away manfully, if hopelessly. Morna went down to her station, concealed from Bertrand by the Blue Rock, a large isolated boulder lying amphibiously, half in the meadow and half in the river. In some ten minutes the fishers found themselves *vis-à-vis* at this point.

"Oh, Mr Cameron! Mr Cameron!" exclaimed Morna, all aghast, "can this possibly be you? Do you really mean to say you've fished down-stream?"

"Conscientiously; every yard of the water," said Bertrand.

"Oh dear! oh dear! how distressing!"

"Distressing, Miss Grant! why?"

"Now, Mr Cameron, I told you my discipline was strict, and I really must scold you; it is for your good, besides. You could never expect, surely, to catch trout fishing down-stream in a day like this?"

"I confess I was far from sanguine."

"Of course not. Don't you know they lie with their heads up-stream? and, with eyes in their heads, don't you think they can see you? Put yourself in his (the trout's) place, and think what you would do if you saw a gigantic engine like a windmill bearing down upon you, flapping its enormous wings; you wouldn't lie quietly still, certainly. You must stalk the trout and let the fly drop before his nose, without any previous hint. So consider yourself scolded for spoiling two of my best pools, and show your penitence by running away back and beginning to fish up-stream."

"I'm afraid I don't know how; I'm not much of a fisher, as I told you."

"Oh, there's nothing simpler; please let me

look at your fly first. Oh, Mr Cameron! how *could* you?" exclaimed Morna, in a tone of pathetic reproach, as she examined Bertrand's tackle; "this tackle would do for a river in Norway—an autumn loch-fly too! Oh! how *could* you? Look at mine;" and she displayed a fly of the tiniest dimensions, and a line half invisible terminating in an almost invisible cast. "And you have no other tackle?"

"Nothing finer, I fear," said Bertrand.

"That is very sad. I'm afraid I can't help you either."

"I had better go on fishing down-stream, I suspect," said Bertrand, "and trust to coming across some strong-minded trout who takes a line of his own and lies with his head down-stream."

"Oh no; I'm very sorry, but I really can't allow you; it would demoralise all my trout. Scotch trout, you know, are exactly the reverse of Scotchmen—the farther north you get, the less cunning they are. That is because we haven't got so many clumsy fishers to disturb our rivers up here, and we have more weak-minded English tourists to beguile than the Lowlanders have. So I'm afraid I must be firm, and not allow you to fish down or even up, with that tackle; but, in the mean time, I'll give you a lesson, and then you can take my rod and try the up-stream system."

"You're very kind."

So Morna began from Bertrand's original starting-place, deftly wielding her limber rod, and deftly throwing her unerring line, so that the fly fell vertically, soft as thistle-down, on the likeliest bits of water. Trout after trout of goodly size and experience rose, and, rising, sank no more. The genius of sport took possession of Morna—an abstraction from all other sublunary matters. Her eye, her attitude, her motions, suggested the concentration of the Indian hunter. Very clearly she had no thoughts to spare for a more apostolic class of capture. She had, indeed, evidently forgotten all about Bertrand; and he, after watching her in silence and with some admiration for a time, began to find it so, and didn't like it.

"Why, you're a regular professor, Miss Grant!" he cried at last, to initiate a conversation.

"Oh, please, hush!" said Morna, holding up one hand without looking round.

"Do you see one?" asked Bertrand, in a powerful whisper.

"Oh, hush! please.

"Why, the fish can't hear that, surely?"

"Yes, yes; hush!"

"What a quaint girl!" thought Bertrand, beginning to whistle for distraction; whereupon Morna looked round with such solemn rebuke in her eyes that Bertrand's music instantly ceased; but, taking out his cigar-case, and holding it up, he mouthed the voiceless question, "May I smoke?" whereon Morna's gravity at last relaxed, and she reeled up.

"I see you are burning to begin," she said, "so I will stop here."

"A fisherman ought to be a Trappist, according to you, Miss Grant," said Bertrand.

"Oh, Mr Cameron! adding to all your other crimes by a pun! Well, I know I'm rather tyrannical, but I warned you fairly. And now you try. I promise you I shan't speak a word. I have—let me see—eleven fair trouts; see if you can beat me. You have the best of the water here, so you ought to, particularly if you wade."

So Bertrand took the water, and began the new system, clumsily enough.

"Less line, Mr Cameron!" cried Morna from the bank.

"Hush!" replied Bertrand, reeling up and making another ineffectual attempt to lodge his fly neatly, and then another, and another, and another, and many more after that, all without success. The system was evidently not to be mastered in a moment; and Bertrand, finding this, began to play all sorts of tomfooleries, throwing lines of fabulous length, stumbling about in the water like a hippopotamus, rebuking Morna out of her own mouth when she remonstrated, and making noise enough to startle the grouse far away up the neighbouring hill. At last his fly caught on a tree, and there was an end of all things.

"If you break my rod, or lose that fly, Mr Cameron, I'll never forgive you!" cried Morna; but after a tremendous amount of stretching and scrambling and shaking of branches, the fly was retrieved, and the rod restored intact to its mistress. "Are you tired of it?" she asked.

"Quite," panted Bertrand. "I've done

very well, I think, for a first lesson. Let us sit down and rest here under this delightful tree, and you shall give me a lecture on the theory of your art, if you will."

"Read Mr Stewart's book on angling; that will teach you better than I can; besides, it is too hot to lecture to-day. But seriously, Mr Cameron, your fishing has been sadly neglected; I hope it is not the same with your shooting, otherwise I fear you will be bored up here."

"That would be impossible," said Bertrand, with the gallant *empressement* of his age and profession.

"Some people have found it very awfully possible."

"I never could be bored here; the air is the elixir of life; the scenery is Elysian; and with company such as—such as the present, for instance, the idea of Paradise is realised."

"But perhaps if Adam and Eve hadn't been a little tired, even in Paradise, we shouldn't have been here."

"Then," said Bertrand, with unthinking irreverence, "I am glad that our first parents were bored in the garden of Eden."

"Hush! hush! hush! you are wicked to say so; and besides" (with deep solemnity) "you are making fine speeches to me, and you mustn't."

"I only spoke the truth."

"Now, Mr Cameron, that is a second offence; after warning too. I'll tell you why I dislike fine speeches—it is because I notice that the people who make them are always the people who laugh most at other people behind their backs."

"Then you prefer silent worship? Always the same mania for silence, I see."

"Why do you suppose I want worship at all? The idea of any one worshipping me!— *me!* How ridiculous you are!" and Morna laughed with the heartiest glee at the notion. "Another reason," she went on, "why I don't like fine speeches is, because whoever makes them to me must consider me very weak-minded if he fancies I believe them; but then I don't think myself weak-minded (not in that way, at least), so I am apt to think *him* weak-minded for not seeing that *I* am not; and so, if you went on making them, and I went on gravely accepting them, you would always be thinking, 'here is a foolish creature!' and I would be thinking of you, 'there is a foolish creature!' which might be very wrong and unjust if the real truth were known; and so we should never know each other properly; and I don't think that is so nice when people are living in the same house for a good while: do you?"

"I perfectly agree with you, particularly when such inducements—no, I forgot, I won't say it; I never was so scolded in all my life."

"Perhaps you are afraid of losing your skill in the art; but I will comfort you. My stepsister, Eila, is coming home soon, and then you will have an opportunity, and a good one; because, in the first place, she is beautiful and —and—charming; and, in the second place, I don't think she will consider any one very foolish for thinking or even saying so. Have a little patience, then."

"No, I shall never make any more handsome speeches; you have frozen the genial current of my soul. I shall take the opposite line, and be abusive. I shall say to your stepsister confidentially, on the earliest opportunity, 'Let us, my dear Miss M'Killop, put things on a proper footing at once. Your sister tells me you expect worship. Now, if you think any one can possibly think you beautiful, in your secret heart you must think him idiotic, because you well know that you are in fact plain; and if I went on making fine speeches to you, and you went on accepting them, you would always be thinking, " here is a foolish creature!" and I would be saying of you, " there is a foolish creature!" most likely *you* are, but I know *I* am not; and therefore there would be injustice to me, and you would never have the respect for me to which I am entitled, which would not be half so nice if I am to be for some time in the same house with you; so, I beseech you, let there be no misunderstanding.'"

"What fun it would be," laughed Morna, "to see Eila's face if you said all this; but I really believe you are angry at my lecture."

"So far from it that I hasten to atone for everything by saying that I quite see you are a strong-minded female."

"Thank you very much; but I don't take that as a compliment."

"Of course not, but then you abjure compliments. You're getting awfully prosy, Miss Grant, do you know?"

"I had better go home, then."

"It would be such a favour—you have no idea how you bore me."

"Good-bye, then," said Morna, springing up.

"Ah!" laughed Bertrand, "you see the fine-speech system acts the best, after all; the reverse drives you away at once. I really must go back to the original plan, because (only I'm afraid I can't express it brutally enough) I should be sincerely sorry if you went away just now; your society — any society, I mean, of course—is pleasant under the greenwood tree. Do, pray, sit down, and I will be as docile or as ferocious, as complimentary or as abusive, as you please."

"But what *has* become of mamma? she ought to have been here ages ago. We ought to go and look for her."

"If we did we should break our tryst at the Blue Rock pool, and inevitably miss her. Let us steel ourselves to endure the misery of a *tête-à-tête* for a few minutes more. Mrs M'Killop cannot be much longer in making her appearance."

"By the by," said Morna, as she resumed her seat, "you will *see* to-day another reason why I dislike fine speeches."

"And that is?"

"In the shape of a gentleman who is coming here, and who is never tired of saying handsome things to me."

"What a foolish creature he must be!"

"How do you know?"

"Because any one who makes fine speeches to you must think you weak-minded, and so forth, and so forth, you know."

"Oh, how tiresome this is becoming! do, pray, let us change the subject."

"No, no; let us go on about the gentleman who is coming here to-day."

"Well, his name is Mr Duncanson, and he is coming."

"So you said; and he says handsome things?"

"Yes."

"And why don't you stop him?"

"Never mind."

"Oh, I beg pardon; of course there must be an exception in such a case."

"Well, I don't stop him, because it isn't

worth while; I don't see much of him, and it would——"

"Make him so unhappy?"

"How very absurd you are! No; because it would do him no good—he is too hopelessly a goose."

"Then you *have* some hope for me?"

"I had, but I scarcely think I have now."

"I am all impatience to see Mr Duncanson."

"I don't think you will like him; he is very conceited and purse-proud. I don't believe you will think him a gentleman. *I* don't think him one; but then I have seen so few people. At all events I know he is quite different from you and Captain Pigott, and gentlemen always abuse other gentlemen who are not in their own style, don't they? People say he is clever, but I think him rather stupid and pompous, and very prosy."

"Is he old?"

"Oh no—quite young. He only left Cambridge two years ago. His father lives near this—at Glen Vrechin; he is immensely rich, and bought the place some years ago—and this is the young laird."

"How long will he stay?"

"A week, perhaps."

"Then I shall have no more fishing-lessons for a week, at least?"

"Why not? You may, if you like."

"Because the 'young laird,' when not shooting, will be naturally anxious to air his handsome observations."

"He shall not go fishing with me, at all events. One has quite enough of him in the evenings—too much."

"Well, I must be attentive while he is here, and try to improve my style. Our next quarter is to be Manchester, and I must prepare my weapons for a campaign among the cotton heiresses."

"Do you believe in mercenary marriages, then?"

"I am a Highlander."

"If you were a true one you would despise them. A true Highlander is too proud for such meanness—you ought to be ashamed."

"Miss Grant, you won't let me finish my sentences. I said 'I am a true Highlander,' and, of course, I was going to add, and 'therefore too proud for such meanness.'"

"But why prepare your weapons for the Manchester heiresses, then?"

"Only to be able to parry gracefully all matrimonial attacks."

"Oh! You expect to be run after?"

"Horribly. There is a tremendous run upon nice officers in the manufacturing districts just now. Trade is so depressed, traders are at a discount. The colonel says he won't let any of the young officers go out without a steady old chaperon—a major or a married captain at least."

"Come away, Mr Cameron, I despair of mamma; let us go home."

"No, no; not yet. I'm going to be serious; and oh, how could I be so stupid as to forget? You promised last night that you would sing me a Gaelic song. Do, pray, sing it now before we go home."

"Oh no, I don't think I can; you are in too light a mood to be sung to. Music always makes me feel serious; and though I may not be able to *make* music by my singing, still I am *feeling* music when I sing. I am possessed by a musical spirit, and so if I saw you looking as if you were thinking absurd thoughts, and ready to say something absurd the moment I finished, the spell would be broken, and I couldn't sing at all."

"No, but I promise to think no absurd thoughts, or do anything to break the spell. Perhaps I am as earnest, in my own way, about music as you are yourself. I know it sobers me at once. Your voice is beautiful (scold me if you like),—it *is* beautiful; I would *be* anything or *do* anything you pleased for a century, if you would only sing all the time. *I* should be under a spell, like Merlin in his oak, only I should be happy."

"In spite of the compliment, I will take your promise as sincere; but if you prove false, my musical spirit will be a grieved and angry spirit, and never reveal itself to you again. On second thoughts I won't sing in Gaelic this time; but I will sing you a song which has just come from the Gaelic—a new translation —and it is a Gaelic air; will that satisfy you?"

"It will enchant me," said Bertrand: and then Morna sang "The Lament of the Water-Spirit." The legend tells how the summer sun has drunk up a mountain stream, and how the spirit that dwelt in it has fled away to a hiding in the clouds; and how the spirit of a neighbour stream, mourning his lost love, goes roaming desolately over all the hills and glens whither the mists of evening used to bring them to their "trystes of delight;" and how, wandering, he utters his lament to all the hills and woods and glens and streams, and to the winds and all flying birds, crying to them for hope and consolation; and how they reply, in sorrowful compassion, that they too mourn and lament, but that until the sky also weeps, the spirit's love can never come again. Then in the refrain the spirit calls passionately on the heavens to weep. The air was wild, but beautiful. It followed the spirit of the words, and gave a second interpretation to their common theme: it found a voice in its wide compass for every phase of the sorrowful passion rehearsed, sweeping up from the subdued cadences of despairing love to the tumult and energy of grief distraught. Morna's voice was equal to it; the theme was evidently one that inspired her, and she rendered every ray and shade with a vividness and intensity that made the performance almost dramatic; so that when she ceased, it almost seemed to Bertrand, who had been carried along in sympathy with the singer's enthusiasm, that the scene had been enacted before his eyes, that those trees around him were the trees that had muttered consolation, and that the stream in whose murmurs the spirit's last pathetic accents had been absorbed. With Morna's first note, the spirit of badinage had left Bertrand, and when she had finished, he said, after a pause,—

"You need have given me no caution, Miss Grant; I never felt a song so much."

"I am very glad you *do* feel it : it is an immense favourite of mine—perhaps my greatest. One does feel so sorry for the poor spirit. The air tells the story without the words ; you might almost have understood it with the Gaelic words, if I could only sing it as it ought to be sung."

"It could not have been better sung."

"Oh yes, it could — far, far better; it sounds so tame when I sing it compared with what it appears to my mind when I only *feel* it."

"Even I have often felt the same myself; but you have less reason than most people to do so."

"I don't think so. Now we are serious, I

won't be so silly as to affect to think that I can't sing—a little—and that I improve, but the more I improve mechanically (if that is the right word), the farther I seem to get from expressing what I feel in music—that is, from satisfying myself. Why is it? The standard always seems to rise as one tries to approach it. It is very distressing. The musical idea in one's mind seems to be a sort of Will-o'-the-wisp, and leaves the power of expression, labour as it will, to scramble in despair behind it, never a bit nearer. I can't explain what I mean, even in words, I know."

"Oh, I understand what you mean; but these are rather the feelings of a composer. You might satisfy yourself, if you were a composer, by fixing your conceptions in writing, and leaving professional artists to interpret them—you finding the idea, and they supplying the mechanical expression."

Morna laughed very heartily at this idea.

"I a composer!" she exclaimed. "You must think me very conceited: my aspiration is much humbler: it is only to interpret other people's conceptions so as to satisfy my own sympathy with them."

And so the conversation flowed on in this altered vein, and the two musical enthusiasts soon found that they had many mutual enthusiasms, and, all about art and the beautiful, and the imaginative, and the transcendental, many conceptions and speculations in common — wild, hazy, half-formed, and only half-consciously entertained, and never before expressed by either, till now that the friction of sympathy slowly kindled the power of shaping them into words. There is an exquisite pleasure in these first essays of the dreamer to fix in words the vague and fugitive thoughts that long have haunted him, to puzzle or delight; and an access of self-appreciation generally accompanies our first efforts to unriddle to sympathising ears *our* portion of those dreams which engage the soul of youth "ere fancy has been quelled;" and no matter how much nonsense is talked — the more perhaps the better. Thus no doubt Morna and Bertrand were highly satisfied with themselves; and that of course made the afternoon pass pleasantly, and therefore swiftly; and it is to be feared that Mrs M'Killop's breach of contract, and consequent absence, was, if not altogether forgotten, neither missed nor commented upon.

But at last the sun gave warning that the day was far spent, and their *séance* was broken up, Morna protesting that she could never have believed that Bertrand cared for such things, or indeed that any one else in the world indulged in such fancies, of which she had been hitherto ashamed; and then she wondered how she had ventured to express them, and feared she had talked a good deal of nonsense, and hoped, with a sudden pause of apprehension, that Bertrand had not been laughing at her all the time; and then Bertrand reassured her, and they went home content; and it is quite certain that Morna never upbraided her mother for not having come to the river. A *tête-à-tête* with a handsome young gallant who talked easily, appreciated at least *one* of her gifts, and sympathised with the mysteries of her dreamland — who had *sympathy* with her — there was the newly found, the great delight!—all this was surely better than her usual bill of fare—a garrulous mamma, a stolid step-father, the woes of the M'Whannels, and the palpitations of the Stock

Exchange. It must have been a pleasant variety. Yet when Morna looked at her comely face in the mirror as she was dressing for dinner, she did not seem pleased, for she spoke to it with mingled asperity and sadness, and said—" Oh, how blowsy and common-looking! Could any one *ever* detect 'the subtle essence of beauty' in you?" The last expression was evidently a quotation from Bertrand, who had got through a deal of fine language in the course of the day; but whether he had anything else to do with the apostrophe, who can tell? Still we know that much may happen and be done in one day's fishing, as Mrs M'Killop said in the morning.

CHAPTER VI.

ON descending to the drawing-room, Pigott and Bertrand found that the party had received its promised augmentation: there was Mr Duncanson, " the young laird " of Glen Vrechin; and there was Mr Tainsh, whom Mr M'Killop had alluded to in the morning. The former gentleman was, as Morna had said, the son of an immensely rich man, a Bombay *parvenu*, to whom, however, Fortune had come late in life by a sudden gigantic *coup* made by his firm "in connection with" cotton. To buy land and found a family is a common aspiration among Scotchmen in his position; it had been Mr Duncanson's life-long ambition, and he betook himself with alacrity to realise it, the moment fortune came.

So he became the Laird of Glen Vrechin—a vast Highland territory, with a princely rental

—and set to work "to make a gentleman" of his son. Unhappily this youth had attained the age of twenty, before the necessity that he should be a gentleman had arisen. He was supposed to have completed his education at a middle-class Scotch school, and was, at the time of his father's access of fortune, perched upon a three-legged stool in a Manchester office, qualifying for "business." These antecedents were untoward; but combined with a deeply-ingrained vulgarity of mind, and an inordinate vanity and natural arrogance, they produced as unpromising as possible a raw material from which to turn out the required article. Old Duncanson, however, had a hazy notion that the thing was to be done by one of two very simple processes. His son must either go into the army or take his degree at the university. These he believed to be infallible manufactories for the article in question; and so he placed the alternatives before his son, who, preferring the gown to the sword, was, after a short probation with a crammer, established accordingly at Trinity College, Cambridge. The son's choice was unfortunate for the object his father had in view.

The army might have done something for him, but, in the little world of the university, like gravitates inexorably to like, and young Duncanson fell naturally into a vulgar, tigerish set, in which his wealth and blustering assumption soon made him a leader; so that all his faults were aggravated, and the last end of that young snob was worse than the first. He had sufficient intelligence to make his degree a simple enough matter; and, it being taken, he had settled down at Glen Vrechin as its future lord, regarded by himself and his father as the glass of fashion and the mould of form.

Mr Tainsh was of a totally different species: he was still a young man, and had inherited from his father an excellent business, that of a solicitor and land-agent or " factor " in the town of A——. The latter, and larger, part of the business was the management of the affairs of country gentlemen—a mysteriously lucrative employment—and by his acuteness and knowledge of the kind of human nature with which he had principally to do, Mr Tainsh had managed to secure pretty nearly a monopoly of the " country-side." He had a hearty manner, a jovial way of doing business, and a popular habit of allowing his clients to become considerably indebted to him; and what with this, and the fact that he was rich, a good sportsman, and not without some rough after-dinner humour, the shrewd fellow had secured an *entrée* almost everywhere—even into houses where his manners might very well have excluded him. The fact that he was unmarried greatly diminished his social disabilities in some quarters, and the fact that he was known to be matrimonially inclined made him doubly welcome in others. Mr Tainsh was conversing with Mr and Mrs M'Killop when Bertrand and his friend entered, and Mr Duncanson, posed on the hearth-rug in an attitude of graceful familiarity, was entertaining Morna. His right elbow, resting on the chimney-piece, permitted his right hand to toy with a clustering whisker, while his left was plunged in his breeches-pocket; his rather splay feet, attired in red silk stockings and shiny shoes, sprawled about in the same spirit of *abandon;* his appointments were quite in advance of the fashion,—all glossy, glittering, and splendid, from the silver buckles on his shoes to the solitary ruby which blazed like " Pendragon " in the foamy fretwork of his marvellous shirt-front. Now he had heard, with the savage's instinctive jealousy, of the arrival of the strangers, and having resolved that " these fellows must be put in their proper place at once, and taught ' who's who,' " he turned to confront them, on their entrance, with a carefully rehearsed mien, in which haughty surprise was supposed to struggle with aristocratic apathy. Mrs M'Killop rose fussily to do the honours, presenting the new-comers first to the young laird, whose bow was a *gauche* impertinence, and then to the factor, who greeted them with rattling familiarity.

" I am delighted to make your acquaintance, gentlemen," he said, " and I hope we'll have some prime sport together. I'm always glad to get hold of officers to shoot with,—you army men are mostly good shots—practice, I suppose — and Mr Cameron, I'm specially happy to meet you. We ought to be friends; there's an old connection—a business one—between our families, as you know, I suppose. And when did you hear from His Excellency ? "

"Not very lately; he doesn't write much, you know," said Bertrand.

"You're right there—kept busy, you see—affairs of state—penalty of greatness. It's a pity, though, that he doesn't come home and settle among us; he's had enough of these colonies, you would say : and a fine place and property lying idle—just clean wasted—at home. You ought to suggest it to him, Mr Cameron ; or you might hint that you wouldn't mind looking after the place for him —keeping the house aired and the game in order, ha! ha! ha! You and I would have some fine days there ; the game's just spoiled for want of shooting ; and there's a cellar, sir —my father used to say—and he had helped your grandfather through many a 'tappit hen' —he used to say of that cellar, 'If you want wine, real wine, the juice of the grape and the best grape, go to Aberlorna, and no call to choose your bin.'" And so on rattled the factor. Pigott meanwhile went up to Morna.

"I hope you had great sport this afternoon, Miss Grant," he said.

"Oh no—very bad ; Mr Cameron, you know, is really deplorably backward in his fishing."

"Is he?"

"Oh yes—sadly so; but it was great fun. I was trying to teach him how to fish 'upstream,' and you've no idea how clumsy and absurd he was."

"I thought fishing down-stream had been exploded in the year 'One,'" remarked Duncanson.

"I suspect Bertrand is too impatient a fellow to be a good fisherman," said Pigott.

"Patience is the sportsman's A B C," said the young laird, dogmatically.

"And I confess," continued Pigott,—"I confess I *do* think fishing a bore—except, of course, under the auspices of a lady fair; that is another matter."

"Well, I would be very sorry if any kind of sport bored *me*," growled Duncanson.

"Perhaps if I was a man, and could shoot and hunt, I wouldn't care for fishing," said Morna.

"Of course you wouldn't, Miss Grant; it's quite a *pis-aller*, and a very dreary one too," replied Pigott.

"What the deuce is a pea's alley?" thought Duncanson, among whose acquirements a knowledge of modern tongues was not included. Then finding he could make no impression by words, he stuck his eye-glass in his eye and began a minute and petrifying inspection of Pigott's personal appearance, commencing with the division of his hair, travelling down his nose, over his shirt-front, and so on to his boots, in the vain hope of finding some weak point on which to rest his gaze with scathing emphasis. Pigott, perfectly aware of the operation, and amused, chatted away with Morna as if Mr Duncanson was a grimacing automaton. Dinner being announced, Mrs M'Killop displayed some hesitation as to who should have the privilege of conducting Morna; (who can tell what contradictory schemes were distracting her maternal brain?) but the young laird had no doubt whatever on the subject, and, swaggering up to the young lady, simplified the matter by coolly appropriating her. But on the whole Mr Duncanson felt discomfited. His first efforts to impress the new-comers had not been satisfactory: neither his loud voice, nor his gorgeous apparel, nor his provincial importance, had had any legitimate effect upon them.

On the contrary, he had a painful feeling that something in the quiet, simple style of the young men had impressed *him*. He resolved, therefore, to ignore them, to devote himself, with the grace on which he prided himself, to Morna, and—just show them. The conversation flowed easily among the other five. Bertrand was a capital talker; so was Mr Tainsh; and Pigott, though reserved, spoke to the purpose when he chose. There was a good deal of talk about military affairs, then about the colonies, which gave M'Killop an innings about wool and tallow, and then followed amusing stories of life in foreign parts, wherein Bertrand shone from his lively skill as a *raconteur*, and the humorous turn which he gave to things in general. All went pleasantly and mirthfully, and Mr Duncanson became sulkier and sulkier, as he saw how well his assistance could be dispensed with. But still he persisted in plying Morna sometimes with clumsy badinage, sometimes with anecdotes of his own personal adventures, wherein bargees, proctors, and "bulldogs" of unrivalled speed and ferocity, had invariably succumbed to his prowess or finesse. In the midst of one of his dreary legends, loud laughter following one of Bertrand's stories was joined in by Morna with a vivacity which told Duncanson her attention had been with Bertrand and not with him, there being nothing to call for special mirth in the passage, "And so old Whewell said to me, 'The next time this occurs, Mr Duncanson, I'll convene you and have you sent down.'"

"I beg your pardon, Mr Duncanson," said Morna, when she had recovered her gravity. "I really do; Mr Cameron's story was so absurd, I couldn't help listening to it. And so Doctor Whewell confined you?"

"No, I was just going to tell you that he didn't, but you seem better amused, so I had better put off my story," growled Duncanson. Morna, catching Bertrand's eye, indicated, by a comical look, that her neighbour was not indulging her with any fine speeches. Bertrand glanced at his lowering face, and thought, "What a sulky-looking ruffian!" Then he said mischievously, across the table, to Morna,—

"Miss Grant, you are looking terribly depressed, even cross; is my break-down as a fisherman still preying upon your mind? It is too bad, though, to visit my sins upon society at large; banish this gloom, I pray you."

"Perhaps," said Duncanson, "if you tell her another of these funny yarns of yours, she will cheer up. The conversation of a poor mortal like me has no effect upon her."

"For shame, Mr Duncanson!" said Bertrand; "sitting beside Miss Grant the mortal should forget his mortality; you should feel like the poet when he sang,—

'Blessed as the immortal gods is he,
The youth who gaily sits by thee.'"

"I don't think you quote it correctly."

"Very likely not; but the sense, you know—the sense is everything."

"Or the nonsense," muttered Duncanson.

"Champagne to Mr Duncanson, Jenkinson; a glass of wine with you, Duncanson!" cried M'Killop, noticing the failure of that gentleman's temper; and then, to change the subject, "What is your father going to do about Craigyewkie's lease?"

"*I've* quite decided that Craigyewkie is not to have it."

"But what does the laird say?"

"The laird does as he's bid, Mr M'Killop;" and the arbiter of Craigyewkie's destiny glared round the table as who should say, "You see I'm a devil of a fellow, and not to be come over by any white man; so look out."

"I'm sorry the old man's to lose the farm," said Tainsh, who, as not "doing" for the Duncanson family, had an opinion of his own in the matter.

"You'd better give him one of your vacancies then; I daresay he might suit some of your employers; he's not the sort for us," said Duncanson, with emphasis on the word "employers."

"I daresay he's not," said Tainsh; "new systems require new men; and a man who's been brought up like Craigyewkie, in the old-fashioned ways that have been going on just the same, time out of mind, in an old-established family, takes ill with the sweeping of a new broom in the old place. I'll take a note of him, though. Thanks to you for the hint. He was a great favourite with the old laird of Glen Vrechin when we were factors on the property." These allusions of the audacious factor did not improve Mr Duncanson's temper, and he remained silent till dinner was over and the ladies had left.

"What was the matter with young Duncanson, Morna?" asked Mrs M'Killop, when they reached the drawing-room.

"I think he was sulky."

"I never saw him so before; had you said anything to him?"

"No; I think he came in a bad temper."

"He used to seem so pleased with you!"

"I can assure you that he was neither pleased nor pleasant to-night."

"You must smoothe him down, Morna."

"Mamma!"

"The best match in the county, child."

"And the very worst temper, I'm sure."

"Pooh! nonsense; we're all cross at times. Do you know I've often thought he had quite a *pongshong* for you."

"It is very much misplaced, if he has; I think he is quite odious, and so underbred. Just compare him with Captain Pigott or Mr Cameron, for instance."

"You should never let yourself speak in that way of a person of fortune. The Captain is very gentleman-like indeed, but we know nothing about him. By the by, how did you get on with the other? with young Cameron?"

"Oh, very well; why did you never come, by the by?"

"Oh, that tiresome M'Kenzie had business for me. Well, was there much conversation?"

"Oh, we talked a little."

"Was he—was he—eh?" said Mrs M'Killop, archly.

"What *do* you mean, mamma?"

"Provoking creature! was he attentive?"

"Oh, very! he carried the basket up and my rod."

"Was that all?"

"Well, you know there was nothing else to carry, except myself—and that didn't seem to occur to him."

"Flippant, bad-toned girl!"

"My dear mother, how cross you are to-night!—nearly as bad as Mr Duncanson;" and Morna retreated laughing to the balcony.

"Yes," murmured Mrs M'Killop, sinking into an easy-chair for her after-dinner nap—"Eila would have had any of them she pleased at her feet by this time. I wish the brat would stay away for a month. But, after all, the uncle *might* marry. Duncanson never took to Eila. Duncanson is a bird in the hand. Duncanson must be smoothed. Acres against blood. Fine things—both the two—but acres best of all." And so she went on, slumber gently stealing o'er her, till her last utterances "acres," "Duncanson," "minx," "blood," "M'Whannel," shaded themselves into a gentle snoring, leaving us, however, no longer in any doubt as to the dominant ideas of the sleeper. The gentlemen came late to the drawing-room. Probably the host had exerted himself to soothe Duncanson's dark spirit, or the claret had had a remedial effect on him; for when the party entered, much of the gloom had vanished from his brow, and he was conversing quite affably with M'Killop upon such parochial themes as make the boldest of us tremble, once fairly lodged upon the *tapis* in a country conclave.

In this altered mood, he at once joined himself to Morna, who sat by the window looking out on the glorious summer evening, and began in an apologetic vein, " I'm afraid I was a little silent and sulky at dinner, Miss Morna."

"Were you? I never noticed it."

"Oh, I'm sure you did; and I'm very sorry for it. The fact is, I had a headache, and the chattering of that—that officer on the other side of the table was rather irritating under the circumstances; but my headache is better now, and I offer my apologies."

"I'm sorry you had a headache; but sit down here by the open window; the fresh air will do you good."

"Thanks," said Duncanson, in high good-humour; "the happiness of sitting beside you will very soon cure me."

"You are very kind, but I must go and make tea; besides, my chattering might interfere with your recovery; there is nothing like perfect quiet and fresh air for a headache;" and, so saying, she left him boiling over anew.

In this mood, he rejected the offer of tea with such loud rudeness that every one in the room observed it.

"Why, your friend is one of the dangerous classes, Miss Grant," said Bertrand, who stood beside her.

"Is that fellow mad?" inquired Pigott of Tainsh.

"He's got the black dog on his back, any way," said the factor.

"Morna has been teasing him," thought Mrs M'Killop, "the perverse monkey! I must bring him round." And, intent upon the soothing system, she rose and sailed up to the window where the fellow sat sulking. "You're thinking so much of to-morrow," she said, jocularly, seating herself, "that you're quite absent. Away among the grouse, I suppose?"

"I wasn't thinking of the grouse," was the short reply.

"It is a beautiful night. You'll have a charming 'Twelfth,' I think."

"To tell you the truth, I don't expect it."

"Oh, I am sure you will; and we expect such a splendid bag from you."

"I advise you not to count upon the bag too much."

"Oh, but we do; we know what you and Mr Tainsh can do; and I believe Captain Pigott and Mr Cameron are both splendid shots."

"Oh, they say they're splendid shots, I daresay; but you'll hear a different story to-morrow night. I never saw men of that style who could shoot."

"Jealous!" thought Mrs M'Killop. "Good!" "Ha! ha! ha! so you don't think the military can shoot? Well, Morna does say that Mr Cameron can't fish. She laughed a good deal at him after dinner; but then I don't think either of them is much in her style."

"She seems to listen with a good deal of interest to that tallow-faced gentleman, I think."

"Tallow-faced! ha! ha! what ideas you have, to be sure! Well, perhaps he *is* a *leetle* to the tallowy side. As to Morna, do you know I fear she is making game of him. The dear child's spirits run away with her. The stories she *will* tell of him after! dear! dear! but it isn't right, Mr Duncanson; it is *not* hospitable, and I tell her so, but she doesn't mind me. Now, if you, as an old friend, and more of her own age, were to take a quiet opportunity, and give her a hint, I am sure it would do good, for I'm certain your opinion has weight with her. You see these men are sure to find out she is making fun of them, and then we shall have a disturbance. Will you promise me, now?"

"Really, Mrs M'Killop," replied Duncanson,

much mollified by this new view of the matter, "I don't think your daughter would mind what I said."

"Oh, you don't know, or you pretend not to know, your influence, you sly creature!" and she smote Duncanson playfully with her fan; "but I'll leave it to you and your delicate tact;" and so she went on blarneying the young laird till he rose to the happy thought which Mrs M'Killop had suggested, and embraced it.

"But I'll not interfere," he thought. "I'll let them have their swing of her; that snob Cameron thinks she's spoony on him, I daresay! ha! ha! I'll let him find out his mistake. The confounded supercilious puppy, he thinks he's only got to come down to the Highlands and say, 'Look, and die!' for all the girls to fall down and worship him. Just wait a bit." In which frame of spirit, which did infinite credit to Mrs M'Killop, he forgave Morna, and tacitly vowed himself her ally for the annihilation of the two officers. "I'll just give them a turn of chaff now, to show her I'm up to the game," he thought, and rose to carry out his benign purpose.

The victims were, however, spared on this occasion, for M'Killop remarking that they must be early afoot to-morrow, and that early hours were advisable, the ladies said "good-night," and the gentlemen retired to the smoking-room for "just one."

CHAPTER VII.

Mr M'Killop did not join the smoking-room party, so Duncanson was brought unavoidably into association with his co-inmates. He felt a little awkward and surprised that the others should display perfect unconsciousness on the occasion; forgetting that they were happily innocent of the dark workings of his spirit with regard to them. Their sociable frankness surprised him, therefore, but the indifference it implied made the surprise not altogether agreeable.

"Mr Tainsh," said Bertrand, who had become friendly with the factor, "I can offer you the best cigar you ever smoked in your life."

"Thanks," said Tainsh, selecting one.

"Mr Duncanson, may I offer you one?"

"No, I thank you; I find I prefer my own to any I ever meet. I pay any price for them, you see."

"Ah! you have the pull of me there. I don't think I could afford to smoke cigars if I hadn't a little back-door to get them in by."

"Relations in the trade?" asked Duncanson.

"No, I'm in the trade myself—a sleeping partner in a large firm. Pigott there is one of the principals. We import as a regiment, for the mess, you know."

"Have you a licence?"

"I'll be hanged if I know; perhaps we're smugglers. Are we smugglers, Pigott?"

"You're too rash, Bertrand; the reward is a heavy temptation. What *is* the reward, Mr Duncanson?"

"How should I know?"

"Oh, you seemed to take a strong interest in the matter."

"Confound the fellow! is he trying to draw *me?*" thought Duncanson.

"What is our bag to be to-morrow?" said Tainsh.

"I would be sorry to brag about it till I see it," replied Duncanson.

"I thought there was a great show of birds," said Bertrand; "the keeper says so."

"It's not the birds I'm uneasy about," said Duncanson.

"No! what then?"

"The guns."

"Oh! why so? I suppose you are both good shots, you and Mr Tainsh."

"Oh yes, we're pretty tidy, eh, Tainsh? but we don't know about you."

"I think you may be easy about us," said Pigott.

"Time will show," grunted Duncanson.

"Why shouldn't Captain Pigott be a good shot?" flashed out Bertrand, irritated by the fellow's consistent churlishness. "Most people who know anything about sport beyond their own parish, know that he's among the best of them at Hornsey Wood. As for me, if you don't think I can shoot, back your opinion. I'll back my bag against yours for to-morrow."

"Done," said Duncanson, a good deal surprised by Bertrand's attack.

"What shall it be for?" asked Bertrand; "a fiver?"

"I would prefer a tenner, or a pony still better."

"Oh, a pony if you like."

"A pony, then, done," said Duncanson, and the bet was booked.

"Bertrand, the bet should be for a smaller sum to begin with," said Pigott. "I don't know Mr Duncanson's shooting, of course, but you're a crack."

"Hang it!" cried Bertrand, "I don't want to take advantage of him; if he likes to be off, he *can* be off, or if he likes to shoot for a sovereign, it's all one to me."

"I'm not accustomed to cry off," said Duncanson; "it's more my way to double. I'll double this, if *you're* not afraid."

"You shall—we'll say two ponies?"

"Done."

"What would his Excellency say to these big sums, Mr Cameron?" said the factor.

"As his Excellency won't have to pay, it don't signify to him. You mustn't tell him, though, Mr Tainsh; besides, I mean to win," laughed Bertrand. And Tainsh, who cordially detested Duncanson, heartily hoped he might.

"Are we to shoot in couples?" asked Tainsh.

"Oh yes, it's much pleasanter; and if both the betting guns do, it will make no difference; besides, we shouldn't have men enough for four parties," said Pigott; "and I suppose it will be you, Mr Tainsh, with Mr Duncanson, and Cameron with me?"

"Well, I suppose that will be it; Mr M'Killop doesn't go out himself."

The divan broke up very soon, and the long 11th of August came to an end.

"I think you're sure to win, Bertrand," said Pigott, as they separated for the night; "and I'll be glad of it beyond measure; for of all cantankerous, impossible snobs, your antagonist is the worst."

"Well, I hope I may win. A couple of ponies is more than I can afford to lose, but the fellow's manner riled me so, I would have bet a thousand. Good-night."

The Twelfth of August broke most auspiciously; a thin mist rested at dawn on the hills, down to their very bases; but, when the sun got up, it rose with him, and, as if to temper the heat in the interests of the sportsmen, hung like a thin veil across the sky. Only now and then was there a flash of the sun's unvisored presence, now and then a glimpse of the summer sky's unfathomed blue, as the light tissue of vapour, touched by some current of the upper air, curled away for an instant, to recoil wave-like on the next. The lightest of breezes wavered over the moorlands, not strong enough to shake the dewdrops from the blue-bells nestling in the corries, but greeting the spent climber, as he crested the higher ridges, with a pleasant invigorating breath, and, to pass to the practical, everywhere enough for the pleasant working of the dogs. It was the " very moral of a Twelfth," as Mr Tainsh remarked; and we take leave to think a fine " Twelfth" is the finest and pleasantest day in all the year: clustered round with bright memories of "auld lang syne," and all manner of happy, holiday associations, and still redolent of one early joy that has not departed with the "merry, merry days when we were young," but is still for *us* while we can stem the brae and tread the heather with the spirit of a sportsman, and with the eye to see, and the heart to feel, the great world of beauty lying among the mountains as nowhere else it lies. " Let the huntsman praise his hounds" and stick to his grass country; give us the heather hills and mountain breeze!

The house was a mile or two distant from the point where the shooting was arranged to commence, so the Cairnarvoch party drove thither, starting at 6.30 A.M. It was a day, if ever there was one, to smoothe Care's wrinkled front and soften the asperities of the roughest temper. All the sportsmen were in the highest spirits, for there was every prognostic of a most successful day. Even the young laird laid aside something of his splenetic temper; perhaps the day was too sacred, even in his eyes, not to be celebrated by an armistice, or perhaps the pleasant certainty of winning his bet had something to do with it. Of defeat he never dreamed, for was he not the redoubted shot of the district? and was it likely that he was going to be beat by a muff like this? Why, the walking alone would beat such a lathe of a fellow! He would "collar the swag," as he gracefully expressed it, and he would take Bertrand down a peg at the same time.

"I won't spare him to-night, I can tell him," thus ran his pleasant reflections; "I'll give it him hot and strong, and I'll set Morna on to him; and whether mother Mac likes it or not, he *shall* have it. It's not likely he can afford to pay. These army fellows, with all their swagger, are as poor as rats. Perhaps he'll ask for time! ha! ha! what a lark! and then I might say, 'Oh, by all means! you can settle it by monthly instalments out of your *wages*'—I'd call it wages—' but I won't press you; I can afford to wait.' It would be royal!" These benevolent meditations were broken in upon with an *apropos* by Bertrand.

"By the by, Mr Duncanson, I've been thinking about that bet of ours."

"So have I."

"Well, if you are not quite satisfied about it—that is, if you would like any alteration—I'm quite prepared to meet you: what Pigott said about my shooting last night makes me suggest it."

"It's a little too late in the day, I think. I can't alter the arrangement; it's against all rule."

"Delighted to hear you say so, I'm sure; and now my mind is quite easy about it."

The point of commencement being reached, and a rendezvous for luncheon fixed, and an understanding come to that the bet was to be

decided by the shooting between eight o'clock
A.M. and six o'clock P.M., the parties separated,
and our two friends, attended by the second
keeper (the amiable Mr Campbell fought shy
of them), and with the usual ghillie and pony
retinue, set to work to breast the mountain on
the reverse side of which operations were to
begin. The dogs, though a little wild and un-
steady at first, soon settled down to their work,
and quite vindicated themselves against the
old keeper's aspersions. The birds proved to
be plentiful, and sat in a satisfactory manner,
and Pigott's deadly certainty quite astonished
the keeper and the ghillies. Bertrand was not
so successful; luck seemed to be against him.
The birds *would* rise to Pigott's side, and perhaps he was a little flurried, as the game was
somewhat new to him.

"Bertrand, this will never do!" cried his
friend, after a succession of bad shots, and two
"clane and clever" misses; "what's come over
you? It will never do to let that fellow win
the bet."

"The time hasn't begun yet," said Bertrand;
"but somehow I can't get my eye in; and yet
you remember what my pigeon-shooting has

been since we came home? Would you mind changing sides?" The change was made accordingly, but still the luck remained with Pigott, and still Bertrand was flurried, "tailoring" his birds, and altogether shooting execrably, for him. It was not till well on in the forenoon, about an hour before they reached the rendezvous, that he steadied to his work. In that hour, however, he did great execution, as they traversed a long sunward slope, with the little breeze dancing towards them over coveys of fine size, that sat well and rose nicely —not all in one big brown clump, but right, left, here, there, and everywhere, one by one, two by two—affording shots at all sorts of delightful fancy angles. The last hour Bertrand shot quite up to Pigott's mark; but there had been a lot of lee-way to make up, and when they reached their halting-ground, where the others had not yet arrived, and their respective scores were made up, Bertrand's fell short of Pigott's by a good many brace—the latter attaining the goodly dimensions of twenty-seven brace of grouse, and a few odds and ends, while all that had fallen to Bertrand's gun in the limit of time was twenty brace.

"He must have beat me hollow," said Bertrand. "You know Mr Duncanson's shooting, keeper; and what do you say?"

The keeper was of opinion that the last hour's shooting was quite beyond Mr Duncanson's standard, but that if he had "keepit his temper" he must have walked away from Bertrand's previous performance; "and here they come to speak for thirsells," he added, as the others hove in sight.

"Well, Captain, what have you done?" cried Mr Tainsh.

"I've done very fairly—twenty-seven brace and a blue hare or two; and you?"

"Oh, well enough for me; but that's a tremendous bag of yours; and Mr Cameron—his is the interesting bag—what has he done?"

"Broken down altogether," said Bertrand.

"No? Then you've lost, for Mr Duncanson has shot his best."

"No, no, Tainsh; not up to myself at all—the dogs were shameful. Let's have the count, though," said Duncanson.

The count was made, and Mr Tainsh's score stood nineteen brace, while Duncanson's was twenty-three.

"You've beat me so far, Mr Duncanson," said Bertrand, "and I'm not surprised at it; worse I never shot in my life."

"Do you cap Tainsh's score?"

"Yes; I have twenty brace; so you are three brace ahead."

Duncanson's countenance fell. "I don't think you've so much to complain of," he said; "but I'm disappointed" (he had been shooting at the top of his bent); "I had put myself at twenty-six to thirty. It will be different, though, in the afternoon — the dogs will be better."

Luncheon was quickly enough despatched, and they separated for the second time, the afternoon division of the betting limit being shorter by an hour than the previous half, with all the haste they made.

There was no mistake whatever about Cameron's afternoon shooting; it could scarcely have been beaten. He more than held his own with the redoubted Pigott. The birds were more plentiful than in the morning beats, and everything went splendidly with him till within about three-quarters of an hour of the close, when, calling to the ghillie for more cartridges, it turned out that one of the reserves had been forgotten, and there were none left but "central-fire" cartridges for Pigott's gun, which were useless to him.

"It's all up with me, then," said Bertrand; "awfully disgusting too, when I was doing so well—two ponies gone! and, what's worse, that fellow will have no end of a crow over me."

"Not as things stand, but there's no harm done; take my gun."

"Oh, that wouldn't be fair."

"What humbug!"

"No; in such cases one ought to abide by one's own accidents. I'm shooting a match against Duncanson, and you're not supposed to be here."

"Well, that's an accident in your favour to abide by."

"Much obliged, old fellow; but I couldn't hear of it."

"You're a Quixotic ass! Do you think Duncanson would have any such scruples?"

"Thank heaven, I'm not Duncanson!"

"But for goodness' sake, my dear fellow, do be reasonable. You're picking your own pocket."

"No good talking, Pigott."

"Well, well, take your own way. You deserve to be flogged."

"I may as well stroll home," said Bertrand, and struck off in the direction of Cairnarvoch.

Arrived there, he met Morna on the terrace.

"Good morning!" she cried. "But how do you come to be so early home?"

"I've had such luck—such dismal luck, Miss Grant," and he told her of his mishap and of the bet, and the victory that was now certain for Duncanson.

"Oh, I'm dreadfully sorry; but do you think he really *must* beat you?"

"Oh, certain; he was three brace ahead at luncheon, and he has nearly an hour's advantage of me this afternoon."

"Well, he has no glory at any rate."

"He will think he has, though."

"How odious he is!"

"Perfectly abominable!"

"I will *not* go in to dinner with him again to-day. I wish Captain Pigott or you would save me."

"Let me."

" Oh, if you like."

"I should like it of all things, of course. I'll step forward the moment dinner is announced, and pounce upon you."

" Thanks. Here comes the carriage. Mamma and I are going for a short drive. I suppose you are too tired?"

"I think I must write some letters before dinner;" and they separated.

The shooting-parties returned late. They had been too hurried to count their scores before leaving the moor; and Bertrand went down to see the operation, accompanied by the ladies. Duncanson was in high glee; he had shot a little better, he said, but not at all up to himself yet. He could afford, however, to say something patronisingly civil to Bertrand about his mishap, implying, nevertheless, that some sympathy was due to his disappointment for a tarnished victory.

"'Deed, Mr Duncanson," said the keeper, "ye maunna craw ower crouse till ye see. Mr Cameron shot jist maist uncommon a'thegither, and it'll tak' a heavy bag to beat him for a' his mischance."

The score was told over, and Bertrand's was

found to be twenty-five brace, while Duncanson's was only twenty-one, making Bertrand the victor on the whole day by one brace!

"And ye win for a', Mr Cameron," said the keeper; "and ye desairve it weel; better shootin' I've seldom seen; and ye wad tak' nae advantage."

"I congratulate you with all my heart," said Pigott, "though you scarcely deserve it for your folly."

"I'm *so* glad," whispered Morna to the victor.

"Poor Mr Duncanson!" cried Mrs M'Killop; "where is he?"

But poor Mr Duncanson had flung into the house, muttering, as he passed through the servants, whom the event had drawn into the courtyard, "I should like to know how much Captain Pigott had to do with his score?"

We may be very sure that the sporting event of the day had not mitigated his previous hostile feelings towards Bertrand; and they were worked up to boiling-pitch at dinner-time by the adroit way in which he saw Morna—whom he seemed to look upon as his special property—carried off by that successful gentleman. All the party, thoroughly alive to his bad temper, seemed, by tacit consent, to leave him to himself, except in so far as Mrs M'Killop shot down the table at him, now and then, looks in which sympathy was meant to blend with an assurance that though, for the present, these things were the reverse of joyous, yet splendid opportunities of reprisal were in store for him. The rest of the company were gay and lively, and as Duncanson bent his scowling regard upon Morna, he could detect no satisfactory evidence in her manner, that her next neighbour was undergoing the process of vivisection at her hands, in which he had resolved to be her auxiliary the night before.

"He thinks himself no end of a swell, no doubt. Wait a bit, though. I'll take him down a peg or two before long. See if I don't."

This genial current of thought appeared to promote thirst, and a thirst which was not neglected; but though his potations were conducted on a most liberal scale, they seemed rather to aggravate his sullen humour, which, however, took no aggressive shape till the ladies left the room. When they did so, he took from his note-book a cheque already prepared, and tossed it cavalierly across the table to Bertrand.

"There," he said, brusquely, "that squares our account."

"Oh," said Bertrand, who made allowance for the fellow's feeling a little sore at his defeat, "there's no hurry whatever; perhaps it may be settled without money changing hands. You can have your revenge; it may be your turn next. I shot quite above myself to-day, I confess—this afternoon, I mean."

"It looks like it, certainly. You had nearly two hours less to make your afternoon bag, and yet you beat your morning performance by five brace—the difference is remarkable!—whereas I was shooting better in the afternoon, and couldn't reach my morning score."

"Yes, it was very marked; but we had more birds in the afternoon, and I was shooting above myself,— whereas in the morning I was shooting below myself, and with luck against me. Never mind the cheque now. I'm open to give you your revenge, whenever you like."

"Well, hang me if I shoot you again on the same terms!"

"Why, do you mean that I must be handicapped? how would you do it?"

"Very simply. I would make you shoot by yourself—that would more than equalise us, I think." Then, after gulping down a bumper of wine, he blurted out, "It would prevent mistakes—bags getting mixed, and so on."

Pigott and Bertrand both started to their feet.

"My affair, Bertrand," said the former; "it concerns us equally, but I am senior. And now, Mr Duncanson," he continued, walking quietly round, and confronting the young laird, "you must be aware that mistakes are *not* made, and that bags *don't* get mixed among gentlemen under such circumstances; so I shall take your *immediate* retractation and apology for these words — mark me, *immediate*, or——"

"Gentlemen! gentlemen! gentlemen!" cried M'Killop, rising and trying to get between them.

"Excuse me, Mr M'Killop," said Pigott,

"there can be no interference here. Have the goodness, Mr Duncanson, to say what you have to say at once. Mr Cameron and I are both a little impatient in such matters."

All the wine he had drunk was unable to support the bully thus brought *vis-à-vis* with the catastrophe he had been working up to. Accustomed to hector and domineer with a licensed insolence among his own associates, he had no precedent for being pulled up in this way. Still, but for the depths of his potations, he would not have so far committed himself. His eye quailed, therefore, before Pigott's cool steady look, and he stammered, "I—I—mean no offence; I tell you a bag may get mixed, mayn't it, by the keeper's fault, without the gentleman's cognisance? The keepers may have their own bets too."

"Am I to understand that that, on your honour, is exactly and entirely what you meant!"

"That is all I meant, of course."

"I'm sorry I misunderstood you," said Pigott, resuming his seat; "but I daresay you'll be more explicit on future occasions."

"Oh," said M'Killop, "it was clear to me and Mr Tainsh that no offence was meant. Suspect you and Mr Cameron, Captain! absurd, absurd."

"It was quite clear to Mr Tainsh that the suspicion was absurd anyway," said the factor, drily.

"Well, well," said Bertrand, "Mr Duncanson has explained, and it's all right, and I'll shoot the match singly with you, Mr Duncanson, when you please, and we'll say nothing to the keepers about it."

Cowed and crest-fallen, Duncanson muttered something to the effect that the arrangement would be satisfactory, and that he would name a day before the party broke up. It is doubtful, however, if he ever entertained an idea of throwing good money after bad.

The visit to the drawing-room was short and sleepy. There was no divan in the smoking-room; and over a quiet pipe in their private boudoir, Bertrand and Pigott discussed the events of the day.

"There's no doubt," said the latter, "that we have fallen on our feet in the way of a shooting—a better day's sport I never had in my life; and the dogs, too, are wonderful, and the weather looks as if it would never break, and altogether we've done well."

"It's all very jolly, except that hound Duncanson; he must be simply a maniac," said Bertrand.

"I suspect he's jealous; I think he honours you with that feeling. Probably he is in love with the *fraulein*. No man but a jealous man could have made such an ass of himself as he's been doing ever since he came. He thinks you are in the field against him."

"I don't see how he can."

"Or perhaps he thinks the *fraulein* is too much taken up with you."

"What a vile idea! She's not the least in that style; she's just the sort of girl for a Platonic."

"Is she really?"

"Exactly; she says just what she thinks."

"I see; I had always thought the Platonic form of the disease set in later in life, though."

"She's no end of a nice girl; I like her immensely."

"Duncanson is right, then," said Pigott.

"Platonically, you know," explained Bertrand.

"You had better tell him so; it may save him the trouble of being horse-whipped eventually. He's been playing this game of impertinence ever since he came, and I mean to make short work of him the very first chance he gives me; because he's jealous of you, there's no reason why he should insult *me*."

"If he only knew how she laughs at him and detests him," said Bertrand. "She positively begged that one of us would take her in to dinner to-night to avoid him."

"Oh! the Platonic revelations have reached that stage, have they?"

"There's nothing remarkable in it."

"Poor Duncanson!"

"I don't think you're right about his caring for her, or being jealous; he's only an ill-conditioned provincial."

"Thank goodness he's had to pay for his swagger."

"Oh, the match is a tight enough one; he may win that back again."

"Not he; and what's more, he won't try."

"Think not?"

"Not unless your Platonics drive him perfectly out of his mind."

"What queer notions you have! Well, I'm off to bed."

"Good-night, Plato!"

"Sleep sound, Diogenes!"

CHAPTER VIII.

THE programme of the Cairnarvoch party for the 13th of August had been to shoot over some ground lying near home, not to start till after the family breakfast, and to make a short and easy day of it. The plan was, however, upset, as so many plans of the sort are, in the Highlands, by the weather. The sun had gone down upon the 12th in a blaze of glory, and Ben Scarrig, where his last rays lingered, had signalled from cloudless, glittering peaks all manner of golden promises for the morrow; but a sudden change had set in after midnight, and a mournful tableau it was which met the eyes of the sportsmen, when the inexorable *réveillé* of Hamish M'Erracher roused them from their slumbers. The mountains were swathed in horrible wet blankets of cloud. On the lower hills the pine-trees loomed through stagnant mists with a dejected, blue-devilly aspect. The linn and the swollen river moaned wearily, wearily; but, save for their monotonous lamentation, a dumb and dreary stillness held the air. The rain fell perpendicularly, and in buckets; for there was not a breath of wind, and the motionless clouds wore, in their stolid immobility, the look of that most inveterate class of kill-joys who have " a duty to perform."

Even the terriers, who usually hailed the piper's first note with a storm of rival howling, this morning, with their quaint impressionableness by the weather, only half rose in the various nooks where they bestowed themselves, and with one querulous half-yelp, half-yawn, subsided again, and left Hamish undisputed master of the situation. It was, of course, agreed on all hands that shooting was out of the question; and the party separated after breakfast to do battle with the "enemy" according to their several inclinations. Bertrand and Pigott betook themselves to their private sanctum, where, what with writing letters, loading cartridges, drowsing over the newspapers, abusing the weather, and smoking tobacco, they managed to pass the forenoon well enough.

M'Killop disappeared with Tainsh into the business-room, to discuss the *pros* and *cons* of a certain investment in land meditated by the former: Mrs M'Killop went about her household cares; and Morna, finding that Mr Duncanson was cut adrift, and disposed to inflict himself upon her for the forenoon, made an early retreat to *her* sanctum, leaving the young laird to his own sweet thoughts, and the distraction of a match between his right hand and his left, in the billiard-room.

By these dispositions, when Mrs M'Killop returned to the drawing-room she found it empty; and when, some half an hour later, Mr Tainsh repaired thither from his conference in the business-room, he found that lady by herself; and Mr Tainsh was glad of this, for a *tête-à-tête* with his hostess was exactly what the factor coveted at the time. Rather a desperate expedient for killing a wet day, it may appear at first sight, but Mr Tainsh had something much more serious in view. We know that the public credited him with matrimonial intentions, and the imputation was correct; and it was because it was correct, not merely in a vague, abstract way (beyond which the public did not go), but definitely and concretely so, that he was thus willing to face Mrs M'Killop in her den, prepared even to endure a general parade and "march past" of her shadowy ancestors, from the days when Kenneth, son of Alpin, ruled the land. The truth of the matter is, that the factor's matrimonial aspirations were closely connected with a young lady who has not as yet made her appearance personally on our stage, but who, from certain stray allusions to her, on the part of her step-mother and step-sister, may be expected to be found dangerous to the male sex, when she does make her *entrée*. It is quite certain that Mr Tainsh had found her so. Miss Eila M'Killop had produced a very powerful impression upon him, even at first sight: he had nursed the impression, and subsequent meetings had confirmed it: eventually he had set himself in a business-like way to consider the *pros* and *cons* of the matter; and seeing no prudential reasons why he should not indulge his fancy, he had "concluded" to fall in love with her, and had done so accordingly. That he had received encouragement from the lady, it is not for us to say; but it is very possible that he had. He was by no means ill-favoured or disagreeable in his way: he was reputed rich: the lady had really no substantial reasons for affecting social superiority; and why not Tainsh as well as another? Besides, encouragement by no means implies ulterior consent, as many dear but haggard readers must be too well aware. The neighbourhood of Cairnarvoch was thinly peopled; visitors to the castle were few and far between; and, if a young lady in such a situation, is not to keep her hand in when chance occasions offer, what, pray, is to become of her skill of fence when the foil is exchanged for the small sword, and she wishes to use the latter to the best advantage, in real earnest? So it is very probable that Mr Tainsh had something to go upon; but if it were so, being a prudent man, he was anxious to know a little more about the ground he occupied, before he took action: he was also desirous of securing an ally; and there *were* one or two little matters of finance which, as a man of business, he thought might stand some elucidation. And hence his hardihood in plunging into a *tête-à-tête* with Mrs M'Killop. That lady (who had no suspicion of the factor's views—for Tainsh was a sly dog) was always friendly and cordial to him. Her manner, indeed, was intended to mark that a social Gulf *did* yawn between them, albeit masked as much as was possible, by her gracious artifices of condescension; but Tainsh was happily as unconscious of the Gulf as of her benevolent efforts to ignore it; and hence they met on very easy and pleasant terms.

"Well, Mr Tainsh," she said, as he entered, "and what are *you* going to make of yourself all this ongnweeong day?"

"There is a certain cure for ennwy in your company, Mrs M'Killop, and here I come to avail myself of it," replied the serpentine factor.

"A very gallant speech, Mr Tainsh; but you shouldn't throw away such pretty things upon an old woman."

"If *you* begin to call yourself old, Mrs M'Killop, it will be time for *me* to give up making pretty speeches."

"As if we were contemporaries!"

"Much about a muchness, I should say."

"Oh you flatterer! You can't be forty?"

"No, I'm not quite forty; you have only the advantage of me by a year or two, though, if *you* are."

"*If* I am! As if you thought I was no more than that."

"I can only go by your looks, you know, Mrs M'Killop; and if they won't help you to be more venerable, it is not my fault."

"Bless the man! I might be a grandmother."

"A mere matter of climate. If you come to that, I might be a grandfather."

"Well, all my family are said to wear well. At eighty-nine, my grandmother—Mrs M'Kechnie of Tillywheesle—had a cheek like an apple."

"I can well believe it," said Tainsh, groaning in the spirit.

"She had the M'Cuaig complexion, of course."

"Yes, that would account for it in a measure," said Tainsh, endeavouring, by intelligent assent, to stem the tide of her reminiscences.

"Oh! you've heard of it, then?"

"Heard of it, my dear madam!" and the factor seemed all astonishment that it should enter into the heart of woman to imagine ignorance on *that* point. "Heard of it!" he repeated. "Yes, and I have seen it, too, which is still better," fastening his eyes meaningly on his hostess's cheeks, which suggested something terribly tough and underdone.

"Ah! Mr Tainsh, I'm not what I was; if you had seen me when poor dear Grant first met me, you might have spoken."

"I'm certain I would," cried Mr Tainsh, plunging recklessly across the social Gulf, and interpreting her words as a matrimonial idiom of the provinces.

"I think not, in *your* sense, Mr Tainsh," said the lady, with dignity. "I don't think you would; I was *very* particular."

"Yes, yes, ma'am, justly so; but you see, men *will* be reckless; they won't calculate consequences; they rush upon—upon—eh?—you know."

"There were many such, Mr Tainsh, eligible and ineligible."

"You don't need to tell me that."

"It's not fair to mention names," sighed the lady.

"Perhaps not," Tainsh assented, hopefully.

"Yet there *can* be no harm in saying that Sir Ronald M'Tammy was one of them. He died, you know."

"A broken heart, ma'am?"

"I—I—have my suspicions. They said it was climate and—and bra—; well, well, I have my own sad thoughts at times."

"No moral blame could attach to you, ma'am," said Tainsh.

"Well, Mr Tainsh, if I was guilty, it was unintentionally so. I could blame myself more in the case of Lord ——; but he is alive. I will change the subject, Mr Tainsh, if *you* please."

"Amen," thought the factor, most devoutly.

"And, Mr Tainsh, with all this nonsense you talk about beauty and love-making, and so forth, are you never going to get married yourself? I'm sure you have a good large number to pick from, and many things in your favour."

Mr Tainsh brightened up. "You're very kind," he said, "perhaps you can suggest some one?"

"Well, there's Miss Trotter, the town-clerk's daughter."

"Oh no; she's not in my style."

"Then, there's Miss Gregorson, at the Knowe."

"I couldn't think of her."

"She has £8000."

"Money is not an ob——, at least not my primary object."

"Then why not Bessie M'Alister?"

"She would *never* do."

"Upon my word, Mr Tainsh, you're mighty particular! And her mother was my own father's second cousin."

"Oh, I know the connection would be most desirable, most unexceptionable, but connection and blood are not my—ahem!—my main objects."

"Good heavens, man! what would you have? You won't be satisfied with money, and you turn up your nose at good blood."

"No, no, Mrs M'Killop—not so; but I am a little ambitious: I want beauty and grace, Mrs M'Killop, and refinement; and I'm sure *you* can't blame me for that. Can you think of no one with these qualifications, who wouldn't turn up her nose at a plain, honest fellow?" and he put on a most meaning and insinuating expression.

"I can't blame you, I'm sure, Mr Tainsh, but these qualities are not so common in the country-side."

"I am sure you have not to look very far from home to find them."

"I vow I can't think where I'm to look."

"Suppose you don't look abroad at all, ma'am, but think of some one who—who—some one, I may indeed say, who—that is—upon the whole—who very certainly *does*—hypothetically, of course" (Mr Tainsh had apparently lost his idea, and was groping about for it all over the English language), "still in all essentials identically—call you—call you by the most endearing of names." The idea came at last manfully through the ruck of words.

"Mr Tainsh! Sir! you forget yourself," said Mrs M'Killop, rising like an insulted archduchess. "You forget, sir, certain things—certain points which you should *not* forget, Mr Tainsh. I have very different views for my daughter—very different indeed. She is not going to throw herself——"

"Excuse me, Mrs M'Killop, you quite misunderstand me," cried Tainsh. The social Gulf yawned wide to his perceptions for the first time, but the factor, though respecting himself, was not the man to allow any sentiment of *amour propre* to interfere with an important object; so, instantly suppressing his astonishment and any resentment he might feel, he accepted the idea of the Gulf, and turned it adroitly to his own account.

"You quite misunderstand me, my dear madam; pray be seated, and listen to me."

"You can scarcely have forgotten, Mr Tainsh, the claims which *my* child has to a considerable alliance."

"Oh, no, no, no!" cried the factor.

"On her father's side, you must be aware ———"

"I am perfectly aware of it—I assure you."

"While I need scarcely remind you that, though now depressed,—impoverished,—confiscated,—extinct in the male line,—from not less than three families of immense antiquity on my side, does the child derive some title to hold up her head and look high."

"I know it—I know it," groaned Tainsh.

"Hector M'Cuaig——"

"He was one of nature's nobles, Mrs M'Killop."

"I don't like the phrase, Mr Tainsh; it has a Radical twang to my ears."

"I mean that a mere patent of nobility could have added no distinction to *him*."

"Perhaps not—perhaps not; then Tork M'Whannel——"

"Oh dear!—oh dear!" thought Tainsh, seeing that the entire liturgy was impending; "this must be stopped at any price;" then he went on aloud with great volubility—

"Yes, ma'am, Tork M'Whannel was certainly one of our most eminent men of his day, take him from no matter what point of view; and indeed I have to ask you for some memoranda about him, but not now, for I must hasten to explain that I had no thought of aspiring—of evening myself—to a match with your daughter."

"Indeed, sir!" said the unreasonable female, half inclined to resent Tainsh's deadness to her daughter's charms.

"No, ma'am, I fly lower. I aspire, I admit it, but I hope not too unreasonably. I will ask you to be my confidante; I know I could not find a more judicious one. I feel certain you are my friend, and I could not have a kinder friend. It was to your step-daughter I alluded."

"Miss M'Killop, Mr Tainsh!" At this juncture Mr M'Killop entered the room, and remained for five minutes or so, rummaging about for a book or a paper. The conversation of course dropped, but the diversion was in favour of Mr Tainsh, for it gave Mrs M'Killop time to reflect, to clear her mind of ancestral hazes, and to reflect upon the attitude she would do well, in her own interests, to adopt. Her first idea was that Mr Tainsh was by no means treating the Gulf with proper consideration; he was a good deal too free with his pontooning; he was aspiring to marry the daughter of HER husband, and that seemed a little too strong. Mythical as was most of her pedigree, it was, be it observed, or had become, all gospel to her; and, indeed, she went so very far back for her gentility, that she was safe from any practical disillusionment —about as safe, for instance, as Odin and Thor from any risk of losing their status, by a serious exposition of the untruth of the Scandinavian theogony. But the more practical side of her character soon asserted itself in the matter, and then Mr Tainsh was remembered as a man of substance, well to do, with an improving position, and every prospect of having the means to become one day landowner and laird himself; in any case, he was independent of subsidising. That was so far well; there would be none of the disagreeables of a pauperised connection; but, before and above all, there would be a permanent rectification of the boundaries between herself and her step-daughter. Her personal relations with that young lady had not been satisfactory to her. In the internecine war which naturally rages between two ladies so connected, the issue is generally in favour of the stepmother; it ought to be twenty to one on her, at least. Holding as she does the key of the position, having the arsenals and munitions under her command, and fighting in the name of the acknowledged sovereign, the tactics of the opponent can seldom achieve more than brilliant guerilla successes, and these only for a time. But, in this case, Mrs M'Killop was not satisfied that her victory had been in any sense complete. For one thing, the enemy would not fight, and, avoiding battle, contrived practically to carry everything her own way, by finesse; and thus, while loudest in her professions of affectionate homage to the queen-regent, confounding the politics of that potentate, and making her ridiculous to herself and all her subjects. Not a little did Eila's powers of fascination over the other sex embitter her step-mother against her. Having the match-making propensities of a frivolous and vulgar mind, and being, moreover, the mother of a marriageable daughter, it was intolerable to her, with her very limited field of operations, that every little project and scheme she formed was invariably counteracted by "that minx Eila;" not a whit the less so that it was done in an apparently unconscious and effortless way. The few men who came, saw her, and she conquered; and poor Morna was nowhere. But still the conqueress remained satisfied with the moral results of her victories, declining the only results which would have been a boon to her step-mother. "What would I not give to be rid of her?" had been for many a day the refrain of Mrs M'Killop's daily thoughts on the subject; and the conclusion which five minutes' reflection now brought her to, was in harmony with it—in other words, that, if Mr Tainsh would be good enough to take Eila away, he was very heartily welcome to her, and also to any assistance which her step-dame could give him in the matter. When Mr M'Killop left the room, therefore, she recommenced the conversation, determined to conclude an alliance with the factor; but, at the same time, to indicate the necessity of his keeping to his own side of the Gulf, that alliance notwithstanding.

"It was to my step-daughter, Mr Tainsh, I am to understand, that you alluded in your—your very unexpected communication?"

"It was to Miss M'Killop that I ventured to allude; and I am afraid I appear somewhat bold and aspiring."

"To a certain extent you do, Mr Tainsh," said the lady, torn between her desire to underrate Eila and to preserve her own dignity; "to a certain extent you unquestionably do."

"I feel that I am unworthy of her."

This was exactly what Mrs M'Killop did *not* feel as to Eila personally; so she was again ambiguous. "To a certain extent, no doubt, it would appear so to the world."

"Her graces and accomplishments—even her youth—entitle her, I feel, to more ambitious views; but——"

"There are other considerations, Mr Tainsh, which you seem to miss, but which possibly the world would make more of, than those you allude to. Of course, personally, there is nothing to be said against you, and a great deal in your favour; but you must remember that, however *respectable* your social position may be, respectability in such a case is alway supposed to be understood; and some people have their ideas, Mr Tainsh, as to—as to—I don't well know how to express myself—as to what may appear in this case some inequality."

Her language was sufficiently ambiguous, and Tainsh took advantage of it.

"I freely admitted," he replied, "that her many qualities entitled her to a more ambitious match."

How stupid he was! he *would* keep hammering away about Eila's qualities, instead of devoting himself to Mrs M'Killop's, and to *her* social requirements. It was not to be stood any longer, however, and Mrs M'Killop discarded ambiguity at last. "Well, Mr Tainsh, if you won't take a hint, I must suggest to you that you can hardly look upon yourself as socially the equal of *my* step-daughter."

"I protest——" Tainsh began; he was going to add that the inequality was not perceptible to him, but paused on the very threshold of his mistake, and went on diplomatically. "I protest, ma'am, that, in these days, refined shades, or even strongly-marked shades, of difference appear to be made little of; affluence, respectability, and an improving position, bridge over such difficulties nowadays, with great ease. We have only to look at the upper ten thousand——"

"*I* am not accustomed to look anywhere else, Mr Tainsh."

"Of course not, ma'am; and your own experience must teach you how little is now made in such circles, in *your* circles, I should say, of social disparity, provided there are counterbalancing advantages."

"It is a sadly democratic age, Mr Tainsh, and what you say is very true; but in other respects I am free to admit that you are perhaps entitled to aspire to Eila." She had now placed Mr Tainsh on his own side of the Gulf, and was, for the future, at his disposal.

"Do you think I have any reason to hope?" asked the factor.

"It is impossible for me to say certainly that you have any reason to hope; but I can see no reason why you should *not* hope—and succeed, too—if you play your cards well."

"May I at least hope for your support?"

"Well, Mr Tainsh, I have a regard for you, and what I *can* do I *will* do, but I warn you that my influence is not great."

"Thank you, thank you, thank you. When does Miss Eila return?"

"In a few days."

"Unfortunately, my stay here must terminate to-morrow."

"You shall be asked back next week."

"You're most kind and considerate. I shall never be able sufficiently to thank you." And they cordially clasped hands in ratification of the alliance.

"I spoke," continued Mr Tainsh, when this important pact was concluded—"I spoke of money as not being my primary object."

"It was unnecessary, Mr Tainsh; if all tales be true, it can be no object at all."

"Comparatively."

"Why not say positively?"

"Well, you see, Mrs M'Killop, I am a man of business."

"Coining money;—you all do."

"Yes, but to coin money, money has to be risked; and in marrying, without any selfish motive, the existence of a fortune of—of even modest dimensions, on the part of the lady, is always a comfort to a man of business."

"To most men I should say, Mr Tainsh."

"Yes, but to an unselfish man of business there is an especial comfort in feeling that there is for his wife a provision free from all risks of speculation, and so forth."

"Settlements, I believe, Mr Tainsh, secure all that, and a man who can't make settlements does wrong to marry; and as for speculation, I'm sorry to find you are a speculator. It would be a great responsibility to countenance the marriage of one — in whom — ahem!— interest is felt—with a speculator."

"I don't call myself a speculator, but there are risks in my business, and sudden large calls for money to assist clients, requiring a considerable free capital; and if one had any sort of idea, any sort of approximate idea of what—that is, of the kind of portion——"

"Do you remember what you said about counterbalancing advantages? it seems now that these are melting away; so let me recommend you to wait till you can disengage a sufficient portion of capital for a settlement, before you turn your eyes in a certain direction."

"Then I am to understand that Miss M'Killop's portion——"

"You can understand nothing about it from me, except this, that if you think you are entitled to be mercenary, *I* don't; and I wouldn't countenance 'your views on any such footing. Upon my word, sir, you *do* set yourself up!" And the lady bridled up and snorted a very well-feigned snort of wrathful surprise. Tainsh was beaten; he was in the position of a cabman or other marauder who, having originally obtained more than his due, is thereby emboldened to ask for yet more, and finds himself summarily snubbed and threatened with the police. So he changed his course, disavowed all mercenary motives, and vowed he would be the luckiest of men if he got Eila penniless; and the alliance was restored to its original footing.

While these diplomatic relations were being established in the drawing-room, and while the forenoon was being passed in a kind of theoretical discontent by Pigott and Bertrand in their own premises, Morna was finding it very dull work all by herself in her retreat. Twice had she essayed an invasion of the drawing-room, and twice had the mysterious pause, consequent on her entrance, warned her that its occupants could dispense with her company. Twice had she entered the billiard-room, but only to find it occupied by Duncanson solus, and, with a hurried excuse, she had made off again; for indeed the expression of that gentleman's face was not inviting. In the first place, he was bored with the weather; in the second, with his own society; in the third, he felt that he was being ostracised and neglected; in the fourth, he was full of wrath against Morna for not seizing the opportunity of having a *tête-à-tête* with him when "these interlopers" were out of the way; and if anything was wanting to fill up the measure of his discontent, it was well supplied by the recollection of yesterday's deep discomfiture. When, therefore, within a very short distance of luncheon, Morna again made her appearance in the billiard-room, with the intention of staying there, even *tête-à-tête* with Mr Duncanson, till luncheon released her, she found that gentleman in a very thundery state of mind indeed —a state of mind which had decided him to beat a retreat from the place altogether. "Still alone?" said Morna, entering the room.

"Still alone; and, for your sake, I'm very sorry for it."

"For my sake? Don't you believe in your own unassisted powers of amusing me, then, on this dreary day?"

"*You* don't seem to, at all events, or perhaps I might have had a chance of trying."

"Oh, I have had so many things to do; but I hope you have not been very dull. Mr M'Killop never *can* tear himself away from his letters and share-lists till after luncheon. Mamma and Mr Tainsh are hatching some treason in the drawing-room; but where are the others?"

"The others? oh, I don't know anything about them. The only person I would have cared to see here was yourself, more particularly as I am going away."

"Going away! I thought you were going to stay the whole week. We hoped you were."

"Is that true? did *you* hope?"

"How very cross and rude you are! Why are you going away? and may I ask why you are angry with me?"

"Well, I am—no, I'm not—I can't be angry with *you;* but I can't stand these fellows here —they're not the form I've been used to, I can tell you; and—and my father wished me to come back to-morrow if possible, and though he had a crotchet about not shooting this year till the 20th, this weather will alter his plan."

"And won't you come back again?" said Morna, with instinctive hospitality.

"I think not."

"Then you are going to let Mr Cameron beat you—as to the shooting, I mean—without another trial?" Not a very lucky remark.

"Ah! I forgot that; we can settle that some other time : I *am* positively going tomorrow at any rate. I have written for my dog-cart."

"I am very sorry," said Morna—even Morna the truthful; for all men and women must justify the hasty Psalmist once at least in a lifetime, it is to be supposed.

"Are you really, now?" said Duncanson; "well, if I thought——" "snarl!" went the pipes; "boom!" went the gong; and the six terriers, forgetting their depression in the prospect of a meal, bow-wowed an energetic chorus; and the door opened, and Mr M'Killop walked in, and walked them off to luncheon. At this meal it transpired that Duncanson was going away next day, also Tainsh; whereupon it was moved by Mrs M'Killop that they should both return towards the latter part of the following week, which being seconded by Mr M'Killop, and Morna having said, under pressure of a full-faced stare from Mr Duncanson, "Pray do"—the motion was carried with a slight formal resistance on the part of the invited. Luncheon over, a visit to the kennels and stable was agreed to by the gentlemen; and four of them started, leaving Bertrand, who had gone to his room for a cigar-case, to follow.

It was not, however, fated that he *should* follow; for as he came down-stairs the door of an ante-drawing-room where music took place had to be passed. It was wide open; exactly opposite the door stood a piano; at that piano sat Morna; on it she was playing; and, of course (her back being to the door), all unconscious of an audience, she lifted up her voice and sang. Bertrand softly entered. It was the "Water-Spirit's Lament" she sang.

Perhaps it may have been that she believed herself to be alone, or it may have been the effect of the accompaniment—at all events, the song seemed to be given with even more power and pathos than when it enthralled Bertrand by the river-side. When it was finished she continued mechanically touching the chords of the symphony for a time, Bertrand remaining silent. At last, she looked round, started on finding that she was *not* alone, and, blushing a delightful blush which intensified the expression of her eyes, said,—

"Mr Cameron! you here? I thought"

(surely this could not have been her *second* within an hour?) " you had gone to the kennels."

" I *was* going to the kennels, but the voice of the siren drew me hither instead ; and if she will allow me, here will I remain."

The siren, who had so steadily avoided Mr Duncanson, made no objection, and Bertrand did remain. It would be grossly unfair, however, to weary the reader with what was after all something like a drawing-room repetition of their *tête-à-tête* by the river. There was more music indeed, but there were long pauses between the songs, and pleasant *entr'actes* both grave and gay, wherein considerable art in nonsense was displayed, and not a little nonsense about art; wherein mirth and earnest mingled with sprightly facility in the mutual self-revelations of two frank, fresh spirits charmed with the novelty of the process. Very dangerous sort of work all this, of course, but these two young people did not seem to feel the slightest alarm; and so, while the rain plashed drearily without, and the invisible sun passed westward behind the surly clouds, there was a good deal of brightness and sunshine in the music-room of Cairnarvoch, at all events. Twice, at intervals of an hour or so, Morna had said, "Ought you not to go to the kennels now?" and twice had Bertrand replied, "In five minutes." The third time she made the remark, it was answered by the yell of the bagpipes, the thunder of the gong, and all the inevitable dogs. "The kennels have come to me, it would seem," laughed Bertrand; but Morna started up in amazement and confusion.

"The dressing-gong!" she cried: "I thought it was only—— what a time we must have been here!" and thereupon hastened from the room with a heightened colour. *She* had clearly taken no note of time. It transpired that the four gentlemen had gone for a long wet "constitutional," and as Bertrand was supposed to have missed them, and as Mrs M'Killop (having slept the whole afternoon and wishing to conceal the circumstance) was unaware of the music-room episode, Duncanson had had no means of knowing that Bertrand had been monopolising the young lady to whom he appeared to grudge the attentions of other gentlemen.

The evening passed off without any remarkable incident: a long wet day in the Highlands takes the curl out of the sprightliest: the animal spirits that have been struggling against atmospheric pressure since breakfast, necessarily experience some exhaustion by nightfall. Thus the dinner-conversation was less lively than on previous evenings, and the flow of mirthful anecdote not half so well sustained; and Duncanson, who had obtained undisputed possession of Morna, found that he was able to get a hearing from her, without seeing that her attention wandered to other parts of the table. Therefore Mr Duncanson's temper was reasonably good, and, while he abstained from giving offence to the others, he did his very best to make himself agreeable to his fair neighbour. Her attention was rather suspiciously earnest, and if Duncanson had been a closer observer, even he, following certain shy, quick glances of hers, that at rare intervals sought another face than his, might have suspected that her appearance of interest in the intellectual garbage which he administered was not due to his offering, but, in fact, to some entirely different cause. The truth is, Morna was *distraite*—she may have had a hundred reasons for being so—and she concealed her distraction by an apparent concentration on her neighbour's conversation, or rather on the monologue which he would have dignified by that name. Then the shy glances? Of course they were directed to Bertrand. Naturally enough. Probably she was displeased with him for not offering to save her from her present partnership, or perhaps —— but after all, if it was her good pleasure to be *distraite*, and to glance in such or such a direction, what have we got to do with it? Why pry? One thing is certain, that Bertrand could not be accused of exchanging glances with her; their eyes may have met, of course, but he had got involved in a long discussion with Mr Tainsh as to the feasibility of converting a portion of his uncle's property into a deer-forest; and taking up everything he did take up, with immense energy, he was ungallant enough to be devoting his attention entirely to this topic; so that the eyes he looked into were not those of Morna, but the green orbs of Mr Tainsh, glittering with the light of argument and self-interest. And well they might, for was not Mr Tainsh a lawyer and a factor? And did not Bertrand's proposal amount to the annihilation of six tinkerable and renewable leases, to the suppression of six tinkerable and renewable steadings—to the extinction, that was, of twelve sources of arbitration, legal communings and compromises, besides coveys of annual letters at six-and-eightpence apiece? So the argument was engrossing, and the battle raged between them over the dinner; was revived, after a lull, over the wine; was carried into the drawing-room, raged there intermittently, and finally smouldered out in the smoking-room, among the ashes of the last cigar. In this way Duncanson had again a clear field with Morna, only disturbed by a short incursion on the part of Pigott, who, however, soon retired to mild *écarté* with Mrs M'Killop; and Duncanson was in high delight, for it would appear that in his brutal, abominable, jealous, bearish way, this fellow liked Morna, and might even—— but sufficient for her day be the evil thereof.

She did not seem to have enjoyed her evening so much as her companion probably imagined she had.

He bade " good-bye " to her (as his morning start was to be early) when the ladies retired for the night, and, sinking his voice into a tone of tender confidence, said, "I would not be coming back again next week, if it was not for what *you* said : did you mean it ?"

"Of course I did," said Morna; "I always mean what I say ;" but at that moment she had no idea what she had said.

"Thank you," said Duncanson, gently pressing her hand ; and he went away to the smoking-room radiant, and she to her room not the least radiant, but quite the reverse, and sat at her dressing-table for an hour doing nothing, not even looking at herself (which, for eighteen and *beaux yeux*, is, to say the least of it, abnormal), but apparently thinking hard, and thinking, moreover, hard thoughts both of herself and some other party unknown ; for now and then she muttered with great energy, "How I detest him! how I *do* loathe and detest him!" And again, "How I despise myself! how contemptible I am ! how—oh, dear! oh, dear!" with which interjections she would cover her face with her hands for a moment, and then fall to thinking again.

The days that succeeded the departure of Tainsh and Duncanson pretty much resembled their predecessors. One day fine, and devoted to the slaughter of grouse; the next a gloomy day, set apart for rest and the art of fishing, as understood by Bertrand and Morna, and theoretically, but not much more than theoretically, supervised by Mrs M'Killop, when it was understood that Pigott was not to be of the party; the third wet, perhaps, admirably adapted for a *séance* in the music-room, or half wet and half dry, so as to suit itself to a combination of amusements.

The dinner-table was, on the whole, cheery and pleasant; it lost something by Mr Tainsh's absence, who was both voluble and adaptive, but that was balanced by the absence of Mr Duncanson's moody countenance and the perpetual *gêne* of his difficult temper. Mrs M'Killop did not share the general feeling of relief at his absence; she, indeed, regretted it —poignantly; for though her match-making spirit might have had some consolation in observing the relations that were springing up between her daughter and Bertrand, still she had fairly come to a decided preference for the absent Duncanson, based rather on prudential than on personal grounds. He, as she has already informed us, in her half-awake revelations, was a certainty as to fortune; he was a "bird in the hand," and a bird who had shown no disposition to surrender to the lures of the arch-fowler, Eila; whereas Bertrand was no certainty in any sense, and, moreover, had very soon to be subjected to the test which Duncanson had, for a wonder, withstood. Again, the latter gentleman had demonstrated during his late visit, amid all his unpleasantness—and even by it—symptoms which did not fail to inspire Mrs M'Killop with much more definite hopes than she had hitherto cherished. So, mourning his absence, it was with far from an approving eye that she noted the growing intimacy between her daughter and her guest; and indeed it is to be doubted if anything, save an all-engrossing passion for sixpenny *écarté* which she nightly indulged with Captain Pigott, would have prevented her from personally superintending a certain *tête-à-tête* on the terrace, which, when the weather was fine, a staircase leading from the open drawing-room windows invited Morna and Bertrand to make a considerable portion of their evening's programme.

To neutralise the effects of these promenades, she felt that her own personal presence would have been necessary, for private remonstrance with Morna might, as she expressed it, only "put nonsense into her head;" but *écarté* carried the day, and she left the rest to the chapter of accidents, relying mainly on the shortness of the time during which the danger would subsist.

What happened in these terrace-walks? Was there any danger such as Mrs M'Killop apprehended? That they were agreeable we may suppose, or they would have hardly been persisted in; but perhaps a small fragment of conversation the night before Eila arrived, may throw a little light on the matter.

"I *am* so sorry to go in to-night," said Morna, when, *écarté* concluded, the maternal telegraph was seen to be working at the window.

"So am I," said Bertrand; "I always am; one never can get enough of a real summer night like this."

"And this will be our last summer-night walk, I fear."

"What has inspired you with that midsummer-night's dream?"

"Oh! our little square party — for Mr M'Killop counts for nothing — will be broken up to-morrow, and then back will come Mr Tainsh, and back will come Mr Duncanson, and then——"

"What?"

"Nothing."

"Mysterious."

"Oh no, not the least; I had finished."

"Perhaps you were going to add that Mr Duncanson would insist on joining us; it was my idea."

"How I detest him!"

"He *will* insist notwithstanding; but I daresay we shall be able to induce the whole of them, except the ecartists, to make a drawing-room of the terrace; and so we shall still have summer nights *al fresco*, and, as you don't appreciate Mr Duncanson, we shall be able to save you from a *tête-à-tête*."

"Oh, that would be *quite* different," said Morna, sadly, absently; a tone which she corrected with a rather blundering alacrity, explaining—"I mean that it would be very different if we could—very nice, indeed; but I suspect they wouldn't. Let us go in, I am so tired, and it has become so cold."

Her manner and voice had changed very suddenly, and her impatience to return to the house was so inconsistent with her remark of half-a-minute ago, that Bertrand puzzled himself as to how he could have offended her.

"What on earth do you and the *fraulein* find to talk about, Bertrand, in your numerous *têtes-à-têtes*?" was Pigott's somewhat comprehensive question in the smoking-room afterwards.

"Well, to answer that, I shall be obliged to divide my reply into a good many paragraphs. First Paragraph——"

"No, no; we'll not take such a large view of the subject. I suppose, on the whole, there is a good deal of the old story. I suppose that, in the long-run, the paragraphs tend to the old conclusion and practical application?"

"What do you mean?"

"I mean that I suppose the Platonic theory

has been abandoned and Duncanson disestablished."

"Then you are all wrong—as to the first clause, at least: for, as to the second, she never cared a straw for the fellow."

"The second clause of your answer contradicts the first, for—though, of course, practically I know nothing of such matters—I should imagine it was rather a straining of the Platonic system to exchange confidences of so delicate a nature."

"Well, you see, Pigott, you *are* rather an ass."

"If to be ignorant of that sort of rubbish is to be an ass, an ass let me continue to the end of time. I've often wondered, by the by, that, with all your amazing follies, it has not arrived to you to fall in love before."

"How do you know, pray?"

"Know, my dear fellow? If you had, what a row there would have been about it! what whirlwinds, and tempests, and fiery flames, and desolation! I quite shudder to think how well I should have known about it."

"As we are in an argumentative mood, let me suggest to you that that conviction of yours ought to prove to you that the Platonic system still prevails."

"I don't admit it; everything must have a beginning,—a fever has its initial stages before the crisis comes. Do you mean—do you dare —to tell me that you don't care for that girl?"

"Care for her? Of course I do; but—but —not as you mean. I think she is one of the nicest girls I ever met,—clever, cheery, good-tempered, and——"

"Very fond of me," suggested Pigott.

"I'll be hanged if she is!" cried Bertrand.

"I was speaking in your person, you blockhead; but you help my diagnosis."

"Confound your diagnosis! what are you driving at? Why shouldn't I like the girl as a friend? If it comes to that, why shouldn't I be in love with her, if it suits my convenience to be in love with her? I haven't taken the vow of celibacy. If it amuses you to think I am in love with her, I have no earthly objection; and I don't see why thousands of fellows shouldn't be. She's decidedly pretty."

"Oh, come, Bertrand! Ha! ha!"

"Yes, she is; her eyes are beautiful; when she is animated they *are*—perfectly beautiful;

her hair is the colour of all others I admire; every one will admit that her voice is angelic,—any fool can understand *that*,—and—and——"

"You needn't bellow like a bull of Bashan: I'm not deaf, and I don't object to any amount of admiration provided you don't rehearse it all to me. It will suit my comfort to a marvel if you continue to fancy the Platonic system still working: pray keep the fires banked up, or I know Cairnarvoch will be too hot to hold me. If there *is* one thing more entirely crushing than another, it is to be shut up with a fellow who is in love. I was on detachment with Baker once. I knew the villain was in that state when we went out, and I trembled. I put on my hardest and most unsympathetic manner to dam up his confidences; but it was of no use. The second evening, out it all came, and after that, we breakfasted, lunched, dined, and supped upon Anna Maria. She went with us to parade; she mingled herself with our tobacco; she popped out of soda-water bottles; she came by the post and had to be read aloud —sometimes with tears; she was written upon reams of paper, read aloud, kissed, wept over, and posted. I tried a counter-irritation; I got up a spurious opposition; I decided to have a big name for my goddess, so I selected 'Thomasina,' and I thundered it out with the full strength of my lungs whenever Anna Maria came on the *tapis*. The stratagem was entirely a failure. Baker was a sympathetic fellow; he became deeply interested in Thomasina, and I found that she only gave him additional leverage for hoisting his Dulcinea into notice, besides sorely taxing my powers of invention to keep up the alternate verse in our idyll. So I got recalled to headquarters: I don't think I could have survived another fortnight. You can understand, therefore, that I think this calm phase of yours is much to be commended. Stick to it."

"Keep your mind easy; but as to your saying that Morna is not pretty——"

"I declare it's past midnight," cried Pigott, jumping up, "so I shall go and dream of 'THOMASINA!'"

CHAPTER IX.

A COMING event that is tardy in its advent, and yet perpetually keeps casting forward the shadow of its influence upon other circumstances, holding them, as it were, in a provisional condition, and in a state of suspense, is as worrying in fiction as it is detestable in real life; and therefore we are glad that Miss Eila M'Killop is now going to present herself *in propriâ personâ*, and to give us an opportunity of judging of her on something more than hearsay evidence. We have heard a good deal about her—contradictory evidence, indeed—and we have seen her influence working oppositely in the persons of her step-mother and of Mr Tainsh; and it is certainly high time that she should appear and show us what she really is. At the commencement of the shooting-season she had been away from home for a few weeks, on a visit in another part of the country; and, if her step-dame's wishes could have effected it, her visit would have been prolonged, as we have seen, for not a few weeks to come : and indeed it might so have been, but for the *empressement* with which Mrs M'Killop had, in her letters, begged her, if she was enjoying herself, by no means " to consider *them*," or to think of hurrying home, where of course they missed her sadly, &c. &c. But this manœuvre Eila interpreted in her own way, and the resolution she took from it was rather to abridge her visit. In the interval, however, the Tainsh episode had supervened, and also Mr Duncanson had developed very hopeful symptoms; so that altogether, when the time of her arrival came, her step-mother could face it with fortitude and even without fear—a state of things which would have sorely disappointed Eila if she could only have divined it. The day following the events narrated in the last chapter, was the day fixed for her return, but, as her movements depended upon no public conveyance, it was uncertain when she might arrive; and therefore, as she had not made her appearance when Hamish sounded for dinner, the party sat down without her.

They had scarcely done so, however, when the sound of carriage-wheels announced an arrival, and, shortly after, the butler intimated that it was the arrival of Miss M'Killop. Mrs M'Killop probably felt that the presence of her antagonist might not have a sharpening effect upon her own appetite—over which she watched with a maternal tenderness—and made an effort to have one more meal in peace.

"The dear child," she exclaimed, "will be sadly tired. Jinkyson, send to Miss M'Killop and say that she is on no account to hurry; she can have dinner sent to her by-and-by, if she wishes it."

"Wishes it, Elizabeth!" said Mr M'Killop; "after a thirty miles' drive the child will wish it, it is to be hoped."

"Tut, M'Killop, what a chatter-box you are! She will take hours to dress, you know —won't she, Morna?—and keep us all waiting. Order dinner for Miss M'Killop in the library, Jinkyson."

On this occasion, however, Miss M'Killop did not take hours to dress, for in a minute or two after the order for her relegation to the library had been given, the door opened and she entered—we should rather say glided into—the room. Without a pause to look at the company—without a glance for any one else, as if hurried away by some impulse of passionate devotion for her step-mother, she undulated swiftly up to that lady, threw her arms round her neck, and embraced her with immense effusion, a challenge which was amply responded to by Mrs M'Killop, who, clutching Eila with the hug of a Cornish wrestler, dealt upon her fair face a long series of deliberate kisses, selecting every now and then a new "claim," so to speak, to work upon—first on one side of the nose, then on the other, then under one eye, then on the chin, then on the forehead—and punctuating each kiss with a low murmur of satisfaction, such as a schoolboy may occasionally be observed to emit when employed in consuming some sweetmeat to which he applies the epithet "goloptious."

"Dear child," said Mrs M'Killop, holding her out at arm's-length to recover breath—provisionally releasing her, as a cat might a mouse, but ready to reclaim her on the slightest provocation,—"dear child, how we have missed you!"

"Have you, dear mamma? and so have

I missed you all terribly;" whereupon Mrs M'Killop opened an entirely new set of "claims," and worked them out unmercifully.

" Eila, let me introduce to you Captain Pigott and Mr Cameron," said her father, who seemed to fidget a good deal while these demonstrations were in progress. The gentlemen made their obeisances, and Eila, seemingly aware for the first time of their existence, bestowed on each a smile that might have quickened the pulse of an octogenarian. To Bertrand's eyes, through which we propose to look at Eila, there was presented in her person the realisation of an ideal which fancy had often revealed to him before, in dim but beatific visions, as, sighing for the beautiful, he roamed about the shadow-land of day-dreams. A figure so light, so airy, moving with such an indescribably effortless ease and grace, that it seemed as if the atmosphere dared offer no resistance to a shape so ethereal, but fell back wondering, to make way for the witchery of each new movement.

The beautiful head and face which crowned this sylph-like form were worthy of it. In average faces the power of expression is pretty evenly divided among the leading features, but in Eila's, her eyes seemed almost to monopolise it. It would have been hard to find a sweeter mouth when the eyes were smiling; it would have been difficult to match the delicate outline of the face, or the exquisite chiselling of every featural detail; nothing could be more finished than the contour and *pose* of the high-bred little head, or more luxuriant than the almost embarrassing wealth of her glossy brown hair; but from all these, the attention was at once withdrawn, when her grey eyes flashed upon the spectator from their mysterious depths some look in which all her expressional power was concentrated. Eyes like these might suggest the idea that they would either see too much or tell too much, unless they were under some remarkable control; but this they were, for the expressional centralisation made the control of expression very complete indeed. When in repose, her eyes were habitually half-concealed by their singularly long and beautiful dark lashes, and then her expression was soft, dreamy, and pensive; but, when called into animation, she seemed able to raise or lower these silky veils with the subtlest graduations, so as to reveal the exact shade of emotion it was her pleasure to reveal, and nothing more. Thus, while no face could beam with a franker intelligence, none could be more inscrutable. The bloom of Hebe lay upon her cheek—a bloom of mingled richness and delicacy, which the pure blood of the north cannot supply, and which, in this instance, came by inheritance from a Mexican mother.

Such was Eila M'Killop—a sight to make an old man young. The look with which she favoured the gentlemen on their presentation was quite a study in its way. Her eyes were on this occasion thoroughly unveiled, and, from their beautiful depths, came such a beam of kindly, frank, gracious cordiality, that Bertrand's heart vibrated like the index-needle of a telegraphic machine, and there seemed to strike into his bewildered mind, some vague, dreamy association of a sweet strain of music floating through the rosy air of a still summer morning, amid the exquisite breath of dewy wild-flowers. Even Pigott was not unmoved, for he actually forgot, until it was all but too late—that is, for a full minute—the glass of sherry, with which no well-regulated palate can dispense as an immediate sequel to clear soup.

Morna glanced across the table to see the effect produced by her step-sister. By what law of association was it, that a certain strange, new light upon Bertrand's face, instantly recalled to her her own self-reviled image in the mirror, on the afternoon of that pleasant day when he and she had first sat by the river? and recalled it with a sudden indefinite sense of pain?

Eila having satisfied the cravings of her step-mother's affection, and having done a little business in the same way on her account, with her father and with Morna, seated herself between her father and Bertrand, and proceeded to satisfy the curiosity of her relatives as to her own history, during the last few weeks.

"You have greatly enjoyed yourself, dear child, I fondly hope?" said Mrs M'Killop.

"Pretty well, thanks, dearest mamma." (*N.B.*—These ladies were for ever expressing by lavish terms of endearment the ferocious and truculent feelings which each, *au fond*, cherished for the other.) "They were all so kind, and pressed me so to stay that I could hardly make my escape; but I did long to be home again; so here you have me back to tease and worry you all;" and she favoured Pigott with a three-quarter glance, which seemed to say, "If you are very good and nice, perhaps you shall be teased and worried too; don't despair." But Pigott was not going to let himself be surprised again. He was at that moment earnestly engaged with a splendid piece of salmon, and if he had spoken out the aspiration of his heart, it would have been this: "Oh! if old M'Killop would only produce some of *that* Steinberg!" His eye, therefore, was as dim and responseless as the salmon's on the sideboard; and Eila, recognising intuitively a subject who was to be no subject of hers, said inly, "Here is an oyster." That even this impenetrable mollusc could be turned to her own account, however, in some shape or other, was obviously the young lady's conviction; otherwise why should she have turned upon him the battery of her brightest glances during dinner? why should he have been selected, and Bertrand, who sat by her, left altogether out in the cold?

Pigott, who saw through, or flattered himself that he saw through, everything, by no means allowed his tranquillity or his dinner to be disturbed by his high privileges. "Don't know what her game may be, just at present," he thought; "but it *is* a game: tremendous pair of eyes, to be sure! Salad, please, Jenkinson."

"Had you a large party, Eila?" asked Morna.

"No; a few people came from time to time, and the house was pretty full for the 'Twelfth;' but most of the people were rather stupid. It didn't seem like the 'Twelfth.' The gentlemen didn't seem to care about shooting even; they went out late and languid; they came home early and languid; they must have shot languidly, I should think, from the size of their bags; they were too languid to speak even: then they sat half the night in the dining-room after dinner, but were no better when they came into the drawing-room—in fact, just the same, except that their faces were red, and they fell asleep in their chairs. They were really rather dismal—so different," her eyes seemed to tell Pigott, "from what *you* are, I am sure."

"Poor Eila! you have been quite a martyr," said Morna.

"Oh, quite; I hope you have been more brilliant here?"

"I think we have not been so very languid, at all events; I think we have been very happy."

"You have had people here?"

"Yes, although it is not very civil in you to suppose that that was necessary to our happiness; we have had Mr Tainsh and Mr Duncanson here."

"How unfortunate I am to have missed them!"

"They are coming back, dear choild," said Mrs M'Killop.

"I am so glad—when?"

"I believe the day is uncertain, but very soon."

"I am so glad."

"I didn't know you were so enthusiastic about either of them," laughed Morna.

"Oh, indeed, yes; everybody likes Mr Tainsh, and Mr Duncanson is too singularly rude and ill-tempered not to be interesting."

Mrs M'Killop's crest began to rise. "My dear Eila," she said, "I beg you won't run him down. He is a remarkably clever, intelligent, agreeable, well-principled young man."

"Of course, dear mamma, that only adds to his interest. I am so anxious to get his receipt for being rude, and cross, and agreeable, and stupid, and intelligent, all at the same time, and still equally popular; it would be most useful to me with my shocking temper;" on which score, however, her eyes confided to Pigott that *he*, at least, need have no anxiety.

"She'll tire of all this eyeing before I do," thought that gentleman, turning on her a countenance as expressionless as the dead wall of a cotton-mill.

"Yes, yes, Eila," laughed Morna, "I wish you would get his receipt; you know how we all suffer from your violence."

"Had you great sport on the 'Twelfth,' Captain Pigott?" continued Eila.

"Oh yes, we had an excellent bag."

"And who shot best?"

"Mr Cameron, I think; but it wasn't quite certain—it lay between him and me."

"That is his modesty, Miss M'Killop," said Bertrand; "he really made the bag; my only triumph was beating Mr Duncanson."

Eila turned her eyes on her next neighbour for the first time, only for an instant; but she gave him a full benefit, which seemed to set many powerful eight-day clocks ticking all through his veins; then she dropped her long lashes and said,—

"I hope he bore his defeat well, and showed a great deal of high principle."

"He showed a good deal of high temper at all events," said Pigott.

"Oh, poor fellow! he had lost his money; it was enough to put him out a little," cried Mrs M'Killop.

"Yes, yes," assented Eila; "that certainly was; poor fellow! it was rather *exigeant* of you, Captain Pigott, to expect him to keep his temper, when it is so much less troublesome to lose it, and when he loses nothing by losing it. Principle is a most useful thing—I must really take to it."

"You must have a private *pick* at young Duncanson, I suspect, Eila," said Mrs M'Killop, with swiftly-rising choler. "Has he not been sufficiently devoted, not enough conquered by your *bows ewes?*"

"Mamma, you are the cleverest of people; I am certain that must exactly be the reason. I never thought of it before; nothing else could make me so blind to his merits when you see them so clearly. Now I think of it, he is *not* very civil to me; but then he is always preoccupied; and that is not Mr Duncanson's fault. Somebody else is the real culprit—somebody else should bear the blame," turning her wicked eyes on Morna's blushing face; "and I have been unjust to Mr Duncanson—selfish and unjust."

"You see, gentlemen," snorted Mrs M'Killop, "how exacting this young lady is. If you are not very gallant, you will be having yourselves abused just like poor Mr Duncanson."

"Oh, ungenerous mamma! just when I have made the *amende.* We had a charming picnic, by the by, the other day," she continued, turning the subject, "to such a delightful old castle."

"Dalquhairn, of course," cried Mrs M'Killop; "the oldest property of our ancestors the Parlanes, Morna, confiscated in the '15" (it certainly could not have been at all a paying thing to be an ancestor of Mrs M'Killop's) —"a noble old place—in the family for centuries—for it is quite certain that Fearguish Parlane was killed at the battle of Largs; and if so——"

"And if so, dearest mamma, it is quite certain that he could have had nothing to do with the picnic I was going to tell you about, which was not at Dalquhairn at all, but at another noble old place—Aberlorna Castle. You know it, I suppose?"

"Know it? In the year sixteen hundred and——"

"Yes. Well, it was at Aberlorna Castle—a splendid old ruin hanging on a cliff over the sea, and splendid old woods all round it; and such a beautiful house!—the modern house, I mean—standing in such a situation, with terraces all down to the very shores of the bay. We went in a boat the last half of the journey; and when we turned into the little bay it burst on us quite unexpectedly. On one side you saw the ruin, and on the other the new house—crumbling walls and mossy battlements and ancient woods on one side, and the beautiful bright chateau on the other, with gardens and shrubberies and terraces, all in the most perfect order. Such a contrast you know—'a picture of the Past and the Present in the same frame,' as Captain Fearon said—and the Lorna running down between them, with a little cascade just under the bridge that joins the two sides—a light, airy-looking, iron bridge. I never saw such a lovely place; and fancy its belonging to some stupid old man who never lives there, but is something or other on the other side of the world! If it was mine I could never bear to leave it. I never coveted anything half so much. I wish the proprietor would adopt me, or leave it to me, or something."

"And don't you know who the proprietor is?" asked Mrs M'Killop.

"No—yes, by the by, I *did* hear his name; Sir Richard or Sir Robert something or other."

"Cameron."

"Yes, that was it; and a stupid old creature he must be."

"Sir Roland Cameron, my dear," said Mrs M'Killop, with awful *empressement*, "is the proprietor. He is also the uncle of our friend

Mr Cameron here, who may not like to hear his nearest relative spoken of so lightly."

"Oh, Mr Cameron!" cried Eila, turning on him *such* a look of bewitchingly innocent contrition, "I *do* beg your pardon; but of course, you know, I couldn't possibly know anything about it. I hope you are not dreadfully fond of him. I hope you are not very angry with me?"

The eye-battery blazed into Bertrand point-blank, throwing, as it were, incendiary bombs and all manner of explosives and combustibles right into the centre of his mazed inner consciousness.

"Angry with you, Miss M'Killop!" he stammered; "oh no, that would be something like—ha! ha!—oh no, that would be—wouldn't it? Yes, I assure you, a sort of impossible—ahem—eh? he! he!"

In acknowledgment of which extremely lucid disclaimer of outraged family feeling, and perhaps in pity for it, the eyes were slowly drooped, and Eila went on,—"You know I only called him stupid for not liking his beautiful place, and I am sure you agree with me that he ought to like it."

"I am sure, if it is anything like your picturesque description, he ought to like it."

"What! have you never seen it?"

"N—no, I am sorry to say I haven't."

"Never seen your uncle's place!"

"Never; but now I am all curiosity. I shall certainly go and see it before I leave Scotland."

"You must indeed, and you must go too, Captain Pigott; you never saw anything half so lovely. Do you sketch?"

"In a very small way," said Pigott.

"Oh, then, *will* you do me a favour?"

"With pleasure."

"A *great* favour, though."

"With *great* pleasure."

"Then you must take a sketch of the tower from the bridge, and give it to me; I worked at it for an hour and a half, and could make nothing of it. I shan't be happy till I have a sketch of it."

"I shall be delighted to try; but if you failed to satisfy yourself, I fear I am not likely to succeed in doing so."

"Oh, I know you will"—as if Pigott's appearance alone was conclusive evidence of his eminence in art—"so it is a promise?"

"I am highly flattered by being asked to make the promise, and you may depend upon my doing my best."

Eila thanked him with a sunbeam (Bertrand could have thrown a plate at him for the stolidity with which he received it), and continued her account of the picnic, which had, no doubt, been much like other picnics; but which—described by Eila in her musical voice, with every little incident pointed by her *naïveté*, and her clear, silvery laugh—appeared to Bertrand to have been a festival of unrivalled attractions. "It was wonderfully pleasant," she concluded, "considering how dull and stupid the people all were, except Captain Fearon" (Bertrand felt that the Captain's alleged vivacity did not improve *his* opinion of the picnic). "Nothing would make them laugh; at last that made *us* laugh, and I'm afraid we behaved very ill" (Bertrand was sure Captain Fearon had,—"the snob!")— "and at last I got quite into disgrace; for fat old Mrs Ringwood tumbled into the sea when we were re-embarking, and her daughters screamed and nearly fainted, and Captain Fearon was obliged to go in after her (in shallow water, you know) in his beautiful plum-coloured knickerbocker stockings; and she was so heavy to pull out that Captain Fearon fell under the water, and they both disappeared for a few seconds, and then came up looking so dismal"—here the recollection revived Eila's laughter to such an extent that she was unable to go on for a time—" Mrs Ringwood looking like a great seal, with her brown front off, and Captain Fearon with all his fine curls hanging like string over his nose; so that I laughed till tears ran down my face, and I could not help saying that it put me in mind of the scene in the 'Colleen Bawn,' where Myles jumps into the water after Eilah O'Connor: and Mrs Ringwood scolded me, and her daughters muttered something about 'heartlessness;' and Captain Fearon, who is a great dandy" (ha! ha! Bertrand was glad of that), " was quite cross and sulky, and wouldn't speak to me, although we had been such friends before, so that I was really quite in disgrace; and although I tried, all the way home, to apologise and be sorry, whenever I looked at the two shipwrecked unfortunates I broke down again,—and so ended the picnic; but I wouldn't have missed the drowning scene for anything." And Bertrand, listening to the merry music of her laughter, and absorbing stray fragments of sunbeam as they passed on their way to Pigott, felt that he would like to go to a picnic with her, and behave ill with her, and be in Coventry with her, and even tumble overboard with her (not Mrs Ringwood), although it should be in stockings of Tyrian purple and upper garments of the costliest velvet.

And so the dinner passed off, and the ladies passed away, and, over the wine, Bertrand was very silent, dimly wondering why Eila had taken a sudden antipathy to him (he had felt that she scarcely seemed to notice his existence, and he was unaccustomed to total neglect from the fair sex), dimly wondering why a glance of her eye should make him feel—feel—like—like —hang it! like *that;* dimly wondering if she had made it up with Captain Fearon, and what sort of fellow Fearon was—that is, when his plum-coloured stockings were thoroughly dry, and his hyacinthine locks restored to their normal curl. No glory sat on the insensate Pigott's face for all the bright sunshine that had been playing on it for an hour. Wool was, as we are aware, Mr M'Killop's conversational staple—colonial wool, by preference; and with him Pigott was carding and teasing that lamentable topic, with an unruffled calm which, considering what he had recently been enjoying, was to Bertrand simply inexplicable.

"She *may* hate me as much as she likes," he thought; "but as for seeing anything in Pigott, she can't, you know—simply can't. A capital fellow, of course—a delightful fellow among *men*, when he likes; but as for the other thing—oh no—oh dear, no !—preposterous !"

In the drawing-room, Morna did not seem to be quite in her usual spirits, but that might only have been by comparison with the exuberant gaiety of her step-sister. That young lady had a hundred little bits of airy gossip to tell, a hundred little laughing sketches of her visit and co-inmates to retail, mysteries of dress to unfold, oddities to caricature, beauties to expatiate upon, touching each subject with the lightest of touches, and gliding from one to another with a most facile *espièglerie*. At last her budget was exhausted, and she said, "Now, Morna, I've told you all about myself;

now for your experiences. What have you been about?"

"Nothing particular, Eila."

"Nothing particular? then I suppose our two guests are as stupid as they look?"

"Stupid, Eila? do you think they look stupid?"

"Oh, dreadfully heavy!—particularly the younger one, Mr—Mr—the nephew of the uncle, you know?"

"Mr Cameron?"

"Yes."

"Well, you're quite wrong: he is not the least stupid; neither is Captain Pigott. Oh no, Mr Cameron is not at all stupid—quite the reverse—in fact, he is just——" Morna stopped, conscious that she was blushing, and that her step-sister was looking at her with a half-smile from under her long eyelashes.

"Just what, Morna?" she inquired.

"Just as clever as most people one meets, I mean."

"He is *your* friend, then, of course?"

"We are very good friends."

"Are they sociable?"

"Yes."

"Both of them?"

"Yes—no—I don't know; why do you ask?"

"Because it will make all the difference while they are here. If they are stupid and sociable, so much the worse; if they are nice and sociable, so much the better. *Are* they nice and sociable?"

"Yes," said Morna, laughing; "I think they are nice and sociable."

"They don't look as if they had been chloroformed in the evenings, like the people at Strathinan?"

"No, I think not."

"Well, if they *are* nice, they mustn't be allowed to shoot every day."

"They don't, as it is."

"Then what do they do with themselves?"

"Oh, they walk about, and do all sorts of things."

"Fish?"

"Sometimes."

"That interferes with your monopoly."

"No, I fish too."

"With them?"

"Yes—at least Captain Pigott never fishes."

"You fish with Mr Cameron, then?"

"My dear Eila, what a catechism you are!"

"But you do, don't you?"

"Yes, yes, I do sometimes."

"Then *he* is nice and sociable?"

"I said so before."

"And the evenings?"

"Well, they pass somehow."

"Whist?"

"No."

"Music?"

"Not often."

"What does mamma do?"

"*Ecarté.*"

"Oh, they play *écarté?*"

"Yes—that is—Captain Pigott does."

"And how do you amuse Mr Cameron, or how does he amuse you?"

"We talk sometimes."

"At rare intervals,—I understand. Apropos of Mr Cameron, I am dying to take you to see that beautiful old castle. Suppose we make an expedition there some day soon — next week?"

"Mr Tainsh and Mr Duncanson are coming back, I think, next week."

"Very well, we can take them with us; and

oh, Morna, of course, the very thing—we might get your admirer, Mr Duncanson, to take us there in his papa's yacht; it would be delightful, and make the journey so much shorter."

"Yes, it would be very pleasant—without Mr Duncanson."

"Oh, you ungrateful——. We are just saying, Captain Pigott" (the gentlemen arrived at this moment)—"we are just saying how charming it would be to make an expedition round to Aberlorna some day next week. You see I am quite a fanatic about it. Do you think you will be able to tear yourselves away from the grouse for *one* day—next week, perhaps?"

"It would be charming," said Pigott. "Any day you like to fix."

"Do let us arrange it, then;" and, by the most infinitesimal *soupçon* of a movement, it was suggested to Pigott that he might seat himself by her on the sofa, which he did, stolidly, probably because he knew it was a soft and comfortable seat.

"What *can* she see in Pigott? How the— what the—why the—what *can* she see in *him*?" thought Bertrand, strolling slowly up to Morna, who was sitting, as she usually was, at this point of the evening, by the window, looking out on the terrace.

"What do *you* say to it, Mr Cameron?" she inquired.

"I? Oh, beautiful! perfectly lovely! that cloud—what a tint!—what fleeciness!"

"You seem to be in the clouds yourself, Mr Cameron," said Morna, looking up into his absent face. "I was talking about the expedition."

"Ah, yes—of course, of course."

"And would you like it?"

"Nothing so much," said Bertrand, entirely innocent of the subject on the *tapis*—he was in "the fierce vexation of a dream"—a midsummer-night's dream: that sofa was the bank whereon the wild thyme blew—and there was Titania sitting on it, "sticking musk roses in the sleek smooth head" of Bottom the weaver.

"Even in Mr Duncanson's yacht?" asked Morna.

"Has he a yacht? He's very lucky. I like yachting: and so Duncanson has a yacht?"

"Yes."

"Captain Pigott, are we to have our *écarté* to-night?" cried Mrs M'Killop.

"Certainly. I am perfectly at your disposal," said Pigott, rising and abandoning Titania with the same stolid calm.

"Does this go on every evening?" asked Eila, also rising, and joining the pair at the window. "Isn't it a little *triste?* what do you do?"

"We go out on the terrace. We're going to-night—are we not, Miss Grant?"

"If you like."

"Shall we go, then?" adding, as Eila made no sign of moving, "Won't you come, Miss M'Killop? You have no idea how beautiful the hills look at this time of the evening from the terrace."

"Thanks—not to-night; I believe I am a little tired;" and so Bertrand and Morna went out by themselves. But their walk that night was far from a success. There were silences, apologies, forced random starts into the driest of subjects, again silences, and then more apologies. What could it all mean? It must have been Bertrand's fault, he looked so abstracted and dull; and Morna evidently thought so, for she looked up now and then into his thoughtful face in a simple, questioning way, receiving, however, no explanation. It was very mysterious and unpleasant.

The summer seemed suddenly to have taken to its golden wings and fled. There was a cloud over everything to-night, and a chillness. Was it possible that from so sunny a source as Eila's presence a sudden mistral had come forth, blowing a damp and obscuring haze between two spirits hitherto so congenial? Or whence else had it come?

"I hear Eila singing, I think," said Morna at last, in a painfully flat tone of voice; "and perhaps listening to her would amuse us more than walking here to-night. Shall we go in?"

Listening to *her!* Where was Bertrand's wonted gallant enthusiasm? Why was Morna not assured that only one singing voice, and that her own, could tempt him indoors on such a night, and from a *tête-à-tête* with her? She was not so assured, at all events; for Bertrand only said, "Perhaps you would prefer it—I daresay you are tired;" and they turned towards the house. As they drew near to the windows, the refrain of Eila's song floated to them very distinctly—

"Come back to Erin, Mavourneen! Mavourneen!
Come back, Aroon, to the land of thy birth!"

Very sweet indeed would the lay have sounded to any ears—very sweet, and plaintive, and pleading; indeed the most obdurate Irish absentee might have been half tempted back to face " Rory of the Hills " in deference to such an appeal; but to Bertrand it sounded something more than very sweet, and he walked into the room in a tumult of thoughts betwixt pleasure and pain.

What a heaven upon earth it would be to be addressed as " Mavourneen " by such a voice, in the sunlight of such eyes! Ah! what bliss! But did—was—*could* there be any one so highly privileged? and if so, did he wear plum-coloured knickerbocker stockings? O ashes! O despair! Eila rose the moment Bertrand and Morna entered; nor could she be prevailed upon to resume her seat at the piano. " I am too humble to sing when the *prima donna* is here to sing," she said. " Dear Morna, I have missed your music so much while I have been away; you *must* sing something now—will you, to oblige me?"

"I will try, but I feel sure that I am not at all in voice to-night. I wish you would sing another, first."

"Oh no, I'm too impatient; I can't wait: do, pray, let us have 'Wings.'"

Morna complied, and Eila seated herself on the sofa. And how did it happen? Was it by electricity, by magnetism, by the teaching of some strange spell, that Bertrand instantly became aware that he might seat himself beside her on the sofa, unrebuffed, and even welcome? "How it came, let doctors tell." Morna had scarcely taken flight upon "Wings," before Bertrand had gravitated to the sofa; and instantly there seemed about him—such as came about Launcelot in the castle of King Pelles—"a marvellous greyte clearenesse, that the playce was as bright as though all the torches of the world had beene there;" and in his ears there was a voice as of "the low-tongued Orient;" and when "Wings" had borne Morna to the end of their pathetic flight of touching aspiration, she found that no sympathising spirit had followed on her track. From the sofa came a murmur as of softly-flowing waters, and from the card-table rang a shrill female cry of triumph—"The king! game *and* rubber! Three-and-sixpence, Captain Pigott!" Hereupon the sofa woke up.

"Another! oh, I beseech you for another, dearest Morna!"

"Another, Miss Grant, as the greatest of favours."

But the favour appeared to be too great—at least it was not accorded. There was thunder in the air, Miss Grant verily believed—otherwise, how *could* she have such a dreadful headache?—which made farther vocal effort impossible. There *must certainly* be thunder in the air—Miss M'Killop agreed—full of sympathy and condolence. And then Mrs M'Killop, snapping the clasp of her purse on the evening's winnings, thought that bed was the best place for a headache, and carried the young ladies off; but before they went, and even across their leave-taking, the mistral blew again with double bitterness, not merely floating the damp mist between Morna and

Bertrand, but dropping a sudden cloud-curtain between him and the "marvellous greyte clearenesse," so that it went from him as it came to him, and he was again in the cold, dank darkness—where, however, he seemed to recognise, with an enhanced perception, that Pigott was fearfully deficient in every personal grace and allurement — distressingly so — poor fellow! They had rather a grumpy time of it in divan that night. Bertrand mooned and moped—while, as bad luck would have it, Pigott's spirits were more buoyant than usual, so that he would have conversed gladly; but, failing that resource, so buoyant was he, that he fell back on music. With the ear of an oyster and the voice of a saw, and being only acquainted with about the eighth part of an old schoolboy tune, and words to match, great results were not to be expected from his performance. Still, it is astonishing how far a slight and rather inferior piece of music will go sometimes; and on this occasion Pigott managed, by dint of encoring himself every second minute, to satisfy his own requirements, and eventually to send Bertrand off to bed in a towering passion, by nothing more elaborate than—

> " Pretty, pretty Polly Hop-kins,
> How d'ye do-oo ?—how d'ye do-oo ?
> None the better, Mr Tom-kins,
> Of seeing you-oo—of see-eeing you : "

and then *da capo.*

CHAPTER X.

"It seems the member for the boroughs has resigned," said Mr M'Killop at breakfast, on the morning after Eila's arrival. "I have a letter from Mr Tainsh excusing himself from coming here this week, on the ground that he will be busy electioneering."

"And I have a note from young Duncanson, to the same effect," said Mrs M'Killop.

"Will there be a contest?" inquired Pigott.

"Tainsh doesn't say; I don't think it likely; the boroughs always go the same way, I believe; still one can never tell till the eleventh hour, and so the canvassing and the speech-making must all be gone through."

"What has Mr. Duncanson got to do with the boroughs?" asked Eila.

"Oh, his father has property and influence in Ardmartin."

"What a pleasant canvasser he will make!"

"He has plenty to say for himself, and he's very advanced, and both qualities are popular, in many places."

"What do the people of Ardmartin go in for?" asked Bertrand; "are they Radicals or Tories, or what?"

"Oh, they're Liberal," replied M'Killop—"very advanced Liberals. I should say that no one had a chance there who is not prepared to go considerable lengths."

"I shouldn't have thought Mr Tainsh was in that line."

"That's just one of the faults Mr Tainsh has," said Mrs M'Killop; and then, mindful of her pact, "he has not many, worthy man!—but that is one, and, in my opinion, it is to be regretted."

"Oh, I don't think Tainsh is advanced, or a Radical at all," said M'Killop; "but you see most of his clients are Whigs, and it's his business to be of their way of thinking; but nowadays every one who isn't a Tory is simply a Liberal, whether he's a Whig or a Radical; and so the Whigs are often obliged to support candidates they can't like in their hearts, simply because the Liberal majority in a place happens to be of a Radical turn, and they must either cast in their lot with them or let a Tory candidate win."

"Yes," said Pigott, "the poor Whigs are between the devil and the deep sea—no mistake about it. What are your own politics, Mr M'Killop?—if that is a fair question."

"Well, I'm not much of a politician: but I've always had a Liberal bias—still I don't think that means a subversive bias—so I don't mix myself up with politics at all. I confess I don't altogether understand the policy of either party, and what I do understand I am bound to say that I don't altogether sympathise with or respect."

"Hear, hear!" cried Pigott.

"Is that what you think of them too, Captain Pigott?" asked Eila, who was again apparently blind to Bertrand's existence, in favour of his friend.

"Think of them, Miss M'Killop? I don't like to think of them. Because when I do, I am forced to confess that the Radicals are the best of the lot, and that is enough to break a gentleman's, not to say a patriot's, heart. They have the courage of their opinions, at all events; they are bold and aggressive. If they are dishonest, they are outspoken. They are the weakest party of the three, and yet they are supreme. They stick to their points, and carry them always. They have outflanked and befooled the other two, because the leader of one had a spasmodic conscience and a twisted brain, and the leader of the other had a spasmodic brain and no conscience at all. As for that eternal 'working man,' the political 'working man'—the Radical's fetish—done into plain English, he is a brutal, rapacious savage—a political brigand."

"Oh, Captain!" cried M'Killop, "I can't allow you to say that."

"My dear sir, you are only falling into the prevailing humbug of the day. You know perfectly well that the political 'working man' is quite a recent and very artificial institution, invented on the stump by Mr Bright, developed in these blackguard processions and demonstrations he was so fond of, and now playing the mischief with everything in the polling-booths. Personally, he is the lowest of his class—the mangiest of the flock has become the bell-wether." *

* Captain Pigott might have added, in justice and with

"Hush, hush, Captain!—think a little."

"Think a little! I *have* thought not a little about the matter. Tell me how you test the common-sense, the honesty, the morality, the patriotism, of an individual or a class. Isn't it by words and deeds? Is the 'working man' to be an exception; and if so, how is he to be tested? I protest I can't see—so I stick to my opinion; but I promise to change it if you can show me that he ever gives out a single patriotic sentiment, ever utters a wish or an idea that is not grudging, subversive, impudently selfish, stamped with ungenerous ignorance, and with moral and intellectual degradation."

"But where am I to find all these dreadful things done and said by the working man?"

"Where?—wherever he is, in his political capacity. Listen to him catechising a candidate; look at him mountebanking in procession; observe him at an election, bonneting

---

truth, that the political "working man" is looked upon with no confidence, but rather with feelings of contempt and dislike, by all the industrious and intelligent of the working classes; wherefore it is to be hoped that, as education becomes more widely diffused, the evil influence he is now able to exercise will in proportion be diminished.

the respectable voter, and covering every decent coat belonging to the opposition with his saliva. The Belleville Socialist in Paris is the plant in full flourish of which our political *ouvrier* is a germ; but ours will develop into a grosser, coarser type. It might have been nipped in the bud; a few round-shot down Piccadilly in the teeth of the Park-railing mob would have stopped this infernal revolution. Pray let us change the subject; this is quite enough to destroy any meal; and to destroy breakfast is to assassinate the day."

"Oh, Captain! you soldiers are bloodthirsty politicians. Fire upon her Majesty's lieges! Fie, fie!"

"Certainly, when they disturb the social system and trample on the laws; just as we hang a Queen's liege when he disturbs the social economy by murdering his neighbour."

"What horrible things politics are!" said Morna. "Every one seems to be in a passion the moment they are mentioned. Even you, Captain Pigott, are looking quite terrible at this moment."

"Every gentleman *ought* to feel angry," cried Eila, "just now, when politics are mentioned;

I feel quite as angry as Captain Pigott myself, although I know nothing about the matter, except that all the common people have suddenly changed, and become rude and disrespectful, and discontented and greedy. I suppose that is politics."

"Oh! but, Miss M'Killop," replied Pigott, ashamed of being betrayed into so much heat, " please don't suppose that I'm angry or excited, or anything of the sort. It is a thoroughly selfish age, and I have schooled myself in its doctrines—and so I say, ' What does it matter to me?' I have no land to lose, thank goodness! and I daresay they won't begin to guillotine the fund-holders for a time; and when they do, one surely will be able to find an asylum somewhere between China and Peru. Is that a turkey's egg you've got, Bertrand, you lucky fellow?"

" I—I don't really know; perhaps it is."

" Or a swan's?"

" I—I—perhaps."

" *You* are quite unfit for the suffrage—that's evident."

"Mr Cameron is not so unpatriotic as you say you are," said Eila; " he is thinking of something else; *he* is angry, I am sure. *Are* you angry, Mr Cameron?"

"I? Oh dear! yes, I am angry—very angry—furious," stammered Bertrand, staggered by a sudden fire from the batteries, and looking about as ferocious as a dispirited sheep.

"I think the politics of your family used to be Liberal," said Mrs M'Killop.

"No, no; only for the last two generations. My uncle is a Whig, but I don't fancy he would support the present Government."

"Oh!" cried Eila, "that puts me in mind of our last night's plan—the yachting excursion to Aberlorna—and this tiresome election will put it off; for of course Mr Duncanson won't be able to come till the election is over."

"But is Mr Duncanson indispensable?" asked Pigott. "He would be a great addition, of course; but couldn't we manage to struggle through a picnic without him?"

"No—because I have set my heart upon his yacht; and I don't think we could invite the yacht without inviting him. We certainly shouldn't get it, at least. I suppose even you couldn't manage *that*, Morna? It would be such a boon, though, if you could."

"Still the same *pick* at James Duncanson!" fleered Mrs M'Killop; "there *must* be something rankling."

"Yes, dear mamma, of course there is; we quite settled all that yesterday. But, Morna, do you think you can really do nothing for us?"

"I have no influence with Mr Duncanson; and if I had, I should be sorry to ask a favour of him."

"That brat Eila is going to spoil everything!" said Mrs M'Killop to herself; and then aloud, "Well, if no one will take James's part" (he had mysteriously become "James" of late), "*I* must; and I will say that he is not so ungallant and so selfish as you make out; and whatever Morna chose to ask him he would grant—of that I'm sure."

"There, Morna," cried Eila; "mamma understands him twice as well as any of us, and she must be right. Do petition 'James.'"

Morna's confusion and annoyance became very great. She glanced quickly round the table; her eye rested on Bertrand. What of consolation did she expect to find in his face? She found nothing there, at all events, but a look of blank, moping vacancy; and then answered Eila in a hurried, tremulous voice.

"I wish you would not be so very—teasing."

Her tormentor glanced quickly at her, and seeing that tears were close to the surface, "ceased firing," and said,—

"Then we must have patience till the election is over."

"But there is some gaiety next week to console you, you know," said Mrs M'Killop. "'The gathering.'"

"Is 'the gathering' next week? Oh, of course; I had forgotten. And are we to go to the ball?"

"Certainly; did you not count upon it?"

"I hadn't thought about it; it *is* such a poky little 'gathering,' and the balls are always very stupid; but I suppose we shall survive it. There is no chance of our being over-fatigued—that is one consolation—for there is never any one worth dancing with."

"Upon my word, my dear Eila, you're growing very fine upon our hands! It struck me that some people thought Lord Edgar Swan very well worth dancing with last year."

"I daresay they did: he had on real clothes

—a black coat, you know, and things—and spoke two or three words of the English language, and these were novelties, and so far pleasant; but we can't expect to be always so fortunate."

"You're civil to the present company."

"It is always excepted, mamma dear; and then we can't expect Captain Pigott to dance with us *all* the evening, or" (as if he were quite an after-thought) "Mr Cameron."

"It—would—be too much happiness," Bertrand managed to stammer out.

"Oh, please, don't apologise, Mr Cameron, we are not really very exacting."

"Indeed I am serious;" and any one who saw his lugubrious face must have admitted it.

"Yes, yes; and knowing how sad a thing too much happiness is, you will avoid it, won't you?"

One little blink of sunshine—rather wintry, but still sunshine—flickered for an instant in Bertrand's eyes, and all power of replication left him.

"What is to be to-day's programme, Captain Pigott?" asked Mrs M'Killop.

"Grouse, Mrs M'Killop. The hill to-day —is it not, Bertrand?"

"Ye-es, I suppose so; or, by the by, was it not to-morrow we fixed for Craiginfrioch?"

"Come now, Mr Bertrand, no shirking; you know it was to-day; and, what is more, we ought to start almost immediately."

"Are you going to fish to-day, Morna?" asked her step-sister.

"Yes, I think so. The day looks well for it."

"I think I'll go with you, if you don't go till after luncheon."

"Do come. I'm not going till after luncheon."

"Are you also a fisher, Miss M'Killop?" asked Pigott.

"Oh no; I'm not at all useful."

Bertrand felt that the obvious antithesis ought to be made some use of; but not even by a look could he point to it.

"I can do nothing useful," continued Eila; "but while Morna fishes in her severe and terrible way, I can amuse myself by watching her, and teasing her, and making pictures of her and the equally stern mountains, time about. Besides, the coolest and pleasantest place where one can be in this fiery weather is down by the river; and the very idea that you are scrambling up Craiginfrioch will make it feel all the cooler. Poor people! I pity you."

"On second thoughts let us give it up, Pigott," cried Bertrand, desperately; "it is really rather too hot to-day."

"Nonsense! A man who has soldiered in the tropics cave in for a day like this! No, no."

"It is very unheroic of you, Mr Cameron," said Eila. "I've quite come to the conclusion, by the by, that all sport is a sort of martyrdom, and therefore the greater the anguish the higher the pleasure. Now, next to sailing on an iceberg in pursuit of walruses, I should think that Craiginfrioch on a day like this was almost perfection in the way of real sporting pleasure. You ought not to miss it, Mr Cameron." But as the ladies left the room, a glance of her eye would have been understood by Bertrand, if he had had any understanding, to say, "You know perfectly well that you can't go to Craiginfrioch to-day; in point of fact, I defy you to go."

"Now then, Bertrand!" cried the inexorable Pigott, "let us look alive."

"Well, really, Pigott, do you know I *am* a little seedy. Suppose we put it off? Eh, old fellow?"

"Nonsense! the grouse are eating their heads off. We haven't touched Craiginfrioch yet; the weather may break again; and if it does, you know they must 'pack.' Seedy? that's a novelty, but all the more reason for going; it will be quite cool up there. Nothing like a walk to put you straight. Come along. Here comes old Campbell with the dogs. Allons!"

So Bertrand went sorrowfully with his friend, and as they made their final exit from the house, a voice came like a falling-star from a diaphanous haze of light muslin at an upper window, "Will somebody be very kind and bring me a bunch of white heather? It grows at the very top of Craiginfrioch, and there are so few opportunities of getting it."

Pigott answered in his earthy way, that if they got to the top he would not forget; and Bertrand, veiling his bonnet, was going to cry out—— but he was too slow. The muslin haze was gone before his ideas came, and he went away bitterly; feeling, however, that if he had to visit the highest mountain in the moon, fight its legendary inhabitant, smash his lantern, and kill his dog, the white heather should certainly be Eila's; and at his hand—not Pigott's, nor another's. There are many pleasanter things in the world than zigzagging up a precipitous mountain, with the sun beating furiously on the climber, and the thermometer ranging at, say, from 90° to 100° Fahrenheit, particularly when the footing is exceptionally bad and slippery. The excitement of an occasional "point" goes far, of course, to balance such inconveniences. Still, at best, there is always required, as the Scotch proverb says, "a stout heart for a stey brae." And how then face such an ordeal with equanimity, when a sleepless night has unstrung the climber's nerves; when the pointing of a dog or the flushing of a covey is to him as nought; above all, when his heart is in open mutiny against the upward movement, and, for reasons which are omnipotent with that unruly member, it beats "Retro Propera!" with every pulsation?

Such was Bertrand's case. The sun was very cruel, and Craiginfrioch was odiously steep and slippery; as for sleep, the poor wretch had had none the night before, except a few moments of semi-delirious unconsciousness, a very travesty of nature's sweet restorer. As for the dogs and the grouse, and their pointings and risings, these were but aggravations, punctuated by Pigott's steady upward tramp, and his frequent anathema for the laggard who was for ever behind, and "simply ruining these two young dogs—simply playing Old Harry with two valuable animals." As for Bertrand's heart, we know where it was—down below, in the pleasant meadows, by the cool river, among the shadowy trees, where were flowers, and lingering dew, and grateful umbrage, and where he fancied to himself the vocal pines mingling Æolian murmurs with the warbling of the waters and the dreamy summer-song of birds, and thought how the sweet natural diapason would soon be completed by a music more exquisite still.

But the white heather was above, and Eila's voice (still fulfilling its obvious function as a falling-star) rang in his ears, "Excelsior!"

and so this poor Tityrus, his heart among the groves with Amaryllis, had to dree the weird of a Promethean passion on the rugged breast of Craiginfrioch. Some men glide unconsciously into love; some educate themselves into it; some are lured and surprised into it; and some fall into it, wildly catching at every branch and tuft to save themselves as they slip down the "facilis descensus;" but Bertrand had been seized by a giant power and whirled clear of every obstacle, so that he had fallen sudden, sheer, and prone into that seething whirlpool of troubles. No wonder he was breathless and shaken, and sorely disinclined for Craiginfrioch. When noon was at about its height, he suddenly halted, and cried out to his companion, "Pigott, would you mind waiting a minute or two? I'm awfully thirsty, and I've got such a headache. I see water in that corrie, and I wish to go and drink, and wet my head."

"Go along with you—only, for goodness' sake, look sharp!"

Bertrand went with listless steps towards the corrie, but when within a few yards of it, he stopped abruptly, gazed intently forward to some object down by the little rill, and then, going with a run and a rush and a bound, flung himself upon the ground beside it with a cry of exultation. What was it? "Sunstroke!" said Pigott, and began to descend rapidly from his eminence: but it was rather an antidote to sunstroke; for hermiting there among the cool moist moss and bracken, under the shadow of a dripping rock, nestled one solitary little plant of white heather. There is nothing so cunning as love, unless it be suicidal mania, and Bertrand was all *finesse* and stratagem in an instant. In an instant the hermit had been plucked up by the roots, and thrust bodily into Bertrand's bosom; and when Pigott arrived some moments later, with anxiety in his face, he found his friend laving his forehead with sober earnestness.

"Anything wrong, old fellow?" he asked.

"Beat, Pigott—dead beat!" quoth the serpent, with a splendid simulation of the woebegone in voice and manner.

"You fell, didn't you?"

"Ye-es—a kind of a—sort of a trip; but I'll be better presently; don't mind me, old boy. I wouldn't spoil your day for worlds, and I don't think it would be quite—quite prudent for me to go on. I feel a sort of something—a sort of fuzziness inside my head, you know; but don't stop, I'll find my way home slowly."

"Oh, but I think I had better go with you, Bertrand; you are looking a little queer."

"On no account, Pigott; I should be wretched if you did. In fact I would rather go on than spoil your day's sport. Look! I'm quite strong on my legs again;" and he jumped up with amazing vigour.

"Well, promise me to take it easily, and wet your handkerchief and tie it round your head. Mind you go slow. Better leave your gun with Campbell. I'll take it to him."

"All right—thanks."

"And, by the by," cried Pigott, turning back, "if Miss Thingumbob chaffs you about the heather, tell her I won't forget, if I come across it. I won't go searching for it, though. I hate these humbugging, school-girl crotchets."

"Oh, she wouldn't expect that, you know. *Au revoir!*" said Bertrand, sweetly; and then to himself, "Miss Thingumbob! the savage! Miss Thingumbob! the blasphemer! the abominable! My angel! my star! my——oh!" and he sat down under the lee of the bank, and took out the white heather, and apostrophised it, talking nonsense enough to make angels weep; and then he kissed it over and over again. "She may wear it in her bosom this evening, you know," he explained aloud to all creation, not apparently to the satisfaction of its only animal representative within earshot, a sturdy little Highland cow, staring angrily at him from the other side of the corrie, who stamped her foot defiantly at the sound of the idiot's voice. The distant report of Pigott's gun roused him; he came forth from his lair, and finding that his friend had entirely disappeared behind a shoulder of the hill, began, bounding like the roe, to descend to the valley. Craiginfrioch was the hill which rose immediately behind the house, and as it was very steep, the time occupied in its ascent was great compared with the amount of ground got over. Not so, however, with the descent, especially when accomplished in Love's seven-league boots, in which Bertrand travelled, ignoring all obstacles with the recklessness of young Lochinvar, and only not swimming across the river below, because, here more fortunate than Lochinvar, he found a ford. That having been crossed, there was only an ascent of a few hundred yards, and then the house. Cairnarvoch, by the by, was by this time scarcely a mere "house;" it was an "Abode" at the very least, and was rapidly developing into a "Bower;" Mrs M'Killop constituting the chief obstacle to its being immediately advanced to that position.

The Abode being thus, so to speak, "within hail," and the ascent being singularly precipitous, the first circumstance suggested to Bertrand the question, "Why am I here?" and the second gave him time to ponder it. Fears and tremors came over him. Why had he come here? because *she* was here; there was no sort of difficulty about that, at all events. But then that must be kept a secret—a dead secret—for she hated him—that was evident; still he would love her, and love her, and perhaps, &c. How then account for his return? A slight threatening of sunstroke? Good! capital! but ah! people with slight threatenings of sunstroke generally lie down in dark rooms, with wet things round their heads and their feet in mustard. Women like Mrs M'Killop are always medical; she would certainly understand this system of treatment, and insist upon it; and this was not compatible with angel-worship by the river for the rest of the afternoon, while that other "very agreeable girl" was fishing in the abstraction of her fancy-free meditations.

A sudden call to write an important letter? How would that do? No, that wouldn't do. The telegraphic system did not as yet embrace the summits of Craiginfrioch; and if it did, the post did not go out till to-morrow morning.

Despair! what was to be done? Perhaps he had better go up the hill again? Impossible. What then? So there he stood under the ledge of the terrace about a hundred yards from *her*, love and fear fixing him in a stable equilibrium. Suddenly, making him start as if an avenging demon had hissed in his ear, burst forth the strain of Hamish's bagpipes. "Luncheon!" he said to himself, and moved fifty yards farther on. Then he stopped again: luncheon was no excuse; quite the contrary. What was he to do? But, at all events, if they were all at luncheon, he could not be seen from the windows; and thus encouraging himself, he crept up towards the Abode, with all the air of "being on the premises with the intention of committing a felony."

He stopped at the hall-door; sooner than enter it, he would have been torn limb from limb by wild horses. He positively fawned upon Hamish when that minstrel had finished his performance beside him. He wanted moral support, you see: even a very large dog would have been something; and so he button-holed the piper, complimented him upon his playing, asked the name of the air just let off with so much *éclat*, and received a shock on learning that it was known in the musical world as "Give my love brose and butter." Brose and butter! what a revolting class of viands to administer to an angel! The suggestion was coarse and abominable; but Hamish, who was obviously impatient to get to *his* brose and butter, must be detained. Therefore Bertrand said it was a splendid air, and, in short, would the piper accept an encore?

Hamish, being hungry, averred that that was entirely contrary to etiquette; as commuted into a pecuniary shape, however, the compliment was not open to the same objection, as far as he knew, so he accepted five shillings, "for snuff," with surprise and gratitude, and under the influence of these feelings allowed his professional spirit to be roused by Bertrand's compliments and questions, so that he launched into a dissertation on the 376 pipe-tunes in which he was proficient, Bertrand hanging on his words with a pitiable eagerness.

Now, what was Bertrand's plan? What end was to be served by this most idiotic proceeding? and how long did he mean there to remain? It would have puzzled the wretched creature himself to say; and, indeed, has any one, under such circumstances, ever got any plan?

Compassed about as we are with all manner of influencing spirits,—white, black, and grey — that is, good, bad, and indifferent, — it would seem that in such cases all the others give place, and leave Puck and his *confrères* to be the operators of the hour; and a fine time they have of it with their victims, as a rule.

So Bertrand vaguely remained there, talking, or rather listening, to Hamish, with fear and shame raging in his heart.

His back was to the door, but a lover has eyes in the back of his head and an ear in every pore; and after he had been thus engaged for half an hour or so, it needed not the piper's exclamation, "Goot life! here are the leddies!" to inform Bertrand that the luncheon-party, in passing from the dining-room, had turned to the open hall-door, and were standing there at that moment. Deaf to Bertrand's piteous entreaty, "Stop a bit, Hamish; do stop; just one question about the 'M'Intosh's Lament,'" the piper fled, and Bertrand, in an instant, was overboard without a cork-jacket.

"Mr Cameron! where have *you* dropped from?" The voice was the voice of Mrs M'Killop, and perforce he turned towards it, seeing at first only a luminous mist, in which the huge red face of his hostess seemed to roll about like an intoxicated sun.

"Where *have* you dropped from?" repeated the voice; and Bertrand, slowly approaching the group, forced himself to look steadily at it, and replied, with a sort of asthmatic gasp,—

"From the hill."

"Nothing wrong with Captain Pigott, I hope?"

"Oh no; Captain Pigott is perfectly well, thank you."

"But what *is* the matter? you look very strange; are you ill, or only lazy? Oh dear me, you are quite pale!"

By this time he could distinctly see "his angel," and the other "very agreeable girl," as well as the balance of Mrs M'Killop's body, and had recovered a slight command of his senses. Wherefore it flashed upon him that if he said "lazy," the secret was out; whereas if he said "ill," wet applications and mustard were inevitable.

Here was a dilemma. "Not lazy," he replied—"oh no, not at all lazy; and not exactly ill—in fact well, but——"

"But what? are you faint?"

The very thing; faintness is evanescent; you may fish or worship immediately after being faint. Yes, he was a little faint, he thought.

"Girls, wine!"

The light fled from the hall-door, and Morna went with it; and presently, sitting on the steps, in the cool shade and pleasant draught, while Hebe herself proffered a cup of nectar, and a minor (but estimable) Olympian satellite mixed it with water, Bertrand began to think that he would cheerfully pass the remainder of his existence in a state of chronic faintness, even under the supervising eye of Jupiter Tonans (in petticoats). Eila was bewitchingly sympathetic; she looked at him with all her eyes; and oh! did he feel better now? and oh! would he not put his head against the cool pillar? and oh! mamma, dear, wasn't eau-de-Cologne a good thing? and oh! she would run and get some; and oh! she went, and brought back and poured on his handkerchief a subtle, beatified essence, surely expressed from no earthly rind. And then the hypocrite tried to *look* faint (we can imagine with what results), and kept on being only "a little better" for a rather unreasonable time, during which, Morna having said at first (drily, Bertrand thought) she was sorry he felt ill, said nothing more, and eventually went away (very unfeelingly, and so unlike "his angel") to get ready for fishing, which recalled Bertrand to himself, and he jumped up hale and hearty, with a miraculous alacrity and renovation, announcing that he was "quite well."

"But you must keep within doors," said Mrs M'Killop. (Hang it! she *was* medical.)

"Perhaps I had better; yes, perhaps it would be prudent," quoth Bertrand, on the *reculer-pour-mieux-sauter* principle; and then, "on second thoughts, open air is the best thing; but I'll keep in the shade, of course, and I think I'll just stroll down by the river, where the trees are, and watch Miss Grant fishing, and perhaps throw a fly myself when the sun gets lower."

"Very imprudent, Mr Cameron," said Mrs M'Killop; but Bertrand, hastily retreating "to get ready," avoided further opposition.

A few minutes later he was again in the hall, where he was soon joined by Morna. "Are you really going to venture out in the heat already, after being so unwell, Mr Cameron?" she inquired.

"Oh yes, it was nothing,—a mere passing trifle; and it is such an age since I had a fishing lesson, I could not miss the opportunity."

"An age? why, it was only two days ago."

"Two days ago, Miss Grant! absurd! why, it is——" Bertrand stopped short. It was an age to him, for he had lived a decade in the last twenty-four hours; but as a mere matter of fact, Miss Grant was correct. "I believe you *are* right," he went on; "I can't think how I had forgotten. Yes, of course, it was the day before yesterday. Still an opportunity is an opportunity; and besides, I've got a new 'spider' from Campbell, which he says is infallible on a day like this."

"We had better start, then, and make the most of it, if you are quite ready."

"Oh, quite — quite; but hadn't we better wait for Mrs M'Killop?"

"She is not coming."

"Oh, I thought——ahem!—but, by the by, Miss M'Killop is coming; it wouldn't be fair to start without her, would it?"

"Unless she has changed her mind since luncheon, she is not coming either; she had quite given up the plan: did she *say* she was coming just now?"

"I—yes—oh, certainly I thought so!"

"Very well, I'll go and ask her." And

Morna went, and presently came back, saying, with Eila's compliments, that Bertrand must have dreamt it. It was much too warm to go out; and she was reading *such* a delicious novel, which could not be parted with before dinner, and then only with a struggle. "So," said Morna, "we had better start, if you are quite ready."

Bertrand having abandoned a half-entertained idea of becoming "faint" again, was ready to go anywhere any one chose to take him, and surrendered himself to gloom and misery — DEEP, DARK, FATHOMLESS. For all his pains, poor man — for all his pains, he might as well have been on the top of Craiginfrioch. She was avoiding him — that was evident. What *had* he done to make himself so obnoxious? And yet ten minutes ago she was full of the kindest interest and sympathy. Ah! that was only by the impulse of her faultless heart! her repugnance had been for the moment curbed by her pure philanthropy —that was all. She would have looked the same looks, and spoken the same words, to the merest costermonger who was fortunate enough to be afflicted with a temporary faintness in her presence. And then, without doubt, she thought he had misunderstood her gentle kindness, so that she was offended, hurt, and a prisoner, this bright afternoon, all on account of his coarse, selfish infatuation. It was certain that her maidenly feeling was outraged; and he had done it. Bertrand did not spare himself: he cunningly devised instruments for his own torture, and used them without mercy. Still came back the eternal refrain, that he would love her, and love her, and perhaps years of devotion illustrated by splendid deeds done for her sake (and of course under her immediate eye), might at last gain for him some slight response from that precious heart, which no mere man could hope to win in its entirety. But at present a darkness that could be felt compassed him round about, as he went away with Morna—a charming companion, we can conceive, for any young lady. Fortunately, perhaps, Morna was not herself conversationally inclined. She, too, had her abstraction.

Just such another day was this as that on which these two had paid their first visit, in company, to the river. It seemed very long ago to both of them. To Bertrand it was a dim passage in a remote and other life; and to Morna, who now recalled it, it suggested the idea of the beginning of a pleasant song that had been interrupted, and was never likely to be taken up again and finished; a song that had promised to be so beautiful, too, that it, and it alone, might have filled her whole life with music. And was it gone? was it really gone for ever and ever? But certain feelings are too subtle for analysis; or, if analysis be possible, too sacred for exposition in words; and so we prefer to spare Morna's inner consciousness any farther contact with the *brusquerie* of our clumsy touches. Mechanically, as it seemed, they turned their steps towards the same part of the river they had visited on that first day; passing the spot where the trees had rung with the water-spirit's lamentations, had echoed their light laughter, and tossed away to the vagrant breeze the eloquent utterances of their still more vagrant fancies.

This historical spot was passed in silence (it is not likely that Bertrand even recognised it, for all the landscape was to him like some blurred *fiasco* of a photograph; and as to Morna—— but we are not going to pry into *her* feelings), and indeed the silence was only broken once or twice in the whole journey from the house to the Blue Rock, and then on this wise.

"Terribly warm!"

"Intensely!"

Five minutes interval.

"Awfully hot!"

"Excessively!"

"Fine fishing will be necessary to-day."

"It will."

Deep meditation on both sides for ten minutes.

"I have everything very fine with me."

"That is fortunate."

Protracted pause.

"This is an African day."

"I can quite imagine that it is *exactly* an African day."

"Campbell's spider ought to do in a day like this."

"It ought."

Ten minutes more for reflection.

"This weather is almost intolerable."

"It is indeed. Here we are at the Blue Rock; shall we keep our usual stations?"

"If you please."

"*Au revoir*, then, and good sport!" and so they separated and began to fish.

Bertrand got into the water, and stalked slowly up mid-stream, looking like a disconsolate heron, throwing his fly to right and to left with mechanical impartiality, but occasionally halting and favouring some special spot with a protracted flagellation, as if he knew of a trout thereabouts who was not to be lured, but might be bullied, into accepting a fly. For about an hour Bertrand continued his watery promenade. The solitude and the stillness favoured reflection—not a trout rose to interfere with it; while the calmness of the sunshine, the silence of the woods, the sleepy aspect of the quiet mountain-side, and the monotonous sing-song of the river, materially assisted in piling up the agony of his troubled thoughts.

Before him, as he gazed into the river, floated two images: one all that was lovely and perfect, but with a sort of celestial anger, chastened by benevolence and sorrow, disturbing the features of the divine countenance; the other of a dark, brutal type, turning, in

Cain-like remorse, from the bright figure which had just dismissed him, with as much scorn and indignation as is compatible with complete purity and elevation of soul.

The dark figure turned again and again, and held up his coarse, swart hands in the attitude of supplication, almost of worship; but the diviner being shook her beautiful head and ever waved him off.

"Oh! is there no hope? is there no hope?" cried Bertrand aloud in his agony.

"Not when you fish without any fly at all," replied a voice (apparently from heaven), with a symphony of silvery laughter.

Bertrand gave a prodigious start, so that he slipped, was half down, up again, down again. Entirely ridiculous. Whence the voice which kept laughing all the time? He looked to right and to left, down into the river, up into the clouds; he saw no one. Was it a dream? No; there at last, in the shadow of the trees, blooming among the flowers, "herself a fairer flower," he descried the speaker. There was "outraged maidenly feeling" surprisingly merry, all things considered.

Turning red, white, and blue by turns, Bertrand reeled up, discovering that his cast of flies was entirely gone; and then, floundering and stumbling, made the best of his way to the bank. "His angel" was sketching some object, between which and the fair artist his clumsy person seemed to be for ever interposing; for she kept craning (if an angel can be conceived to crane) past his edges, laughing and talking, and occasionally putting in a stroke, without ever looking at him.

"You must be very sanguine, Mr Cameron," she said.

"I—I didn't know I had lost my cast; it must have gone at the last throw."

"A large trout, I suppose?"

"I should say so. Oh yes, a very large trout—immense."

"You saw him, did you?"

"Well, no—not quite."

"Perhaps it was a salmon?"

"I daresay it was."

"Or a pike?"

"Very likely a pike."

If she had suggested a dolphin, Bertrand would have cheerfully assented.

"And what are you to do? have you another cast?"

He had a dozen, at the least, in his pocket; but all lovers are indifferent to truth, so he said he had been stupid, and forgotten his book.

"This has been quite a day of catastrophes for you," said Eila, looking round his right edge; and, when he had executed a demivolt to clear her line of vision, instantly discovering that she had to look on the other side, involving a counter-demivolt, and, for a moment or two, she kept him prancing from right to left, like a bear on hot irons. Nothing, however, could be more demure than her expression all the time.

"Yes," replied Bertrand, "and yet not altogether. I am very he—appy now."

"Happy, are you?" (pause to crane); "really?" (pause to pencil); "why?"

Oh, the bewitching unconsciousness! Oh, the simplicity! Oh, the *naïveté!* Embarrassing, though—very.

"Why? ahem! because—hum, ahem!—you see——"

"If you would be so very kind as to move just the least little bit to the left—thanks! Now I see beautifully."

"May I sit down here?"

"Oh, pray do, and then you won't have to trouble moving so often. I fear I'm a terrible fidget."

"It is a pleasure to move when one is—a—a—ordered."

Could anything be more *bête?* and no one could be more conscious of it than the hapless speaker; but Puck ruled the hour.

"That is a very military sentiment."

"Oh, I didn't mean in that sense. I——"

"Are you fond of the army?"

"Yes, I like it very well."

"Have you been in a great many battles?"

"Well, no—not many." He had once marched with his company to *look* at an electioneering row, and be pelted for a couple of hours by Irish patriots at Killygobslithereen.

"A battle must be delightful?"

"Ye-es, it has a wild excitement, which is always pleasant, of course."

"I hope you always gave quarter, and were merciful?"

"I—I really—don't you know—I——"

"Oh, you didn't! I am afraid you are dreadfully cruel and—that tiresome cow will *not* stand still—ferocious. I'm really quite afraid of you."

And then she looked up from her drawing, and looked at him, and beamed and scintillated, so that Bertrand was one all-pervading "tingle" from head to foot.

"I quite despair of getting that foreground right," she resumed, laying down her pencil. "I must give it up, or I shall be cross and disagreeable for the rest of the day."

"Pray let me look at it."

"Oh no, no! not for worlds! I know you are terribly critical and severe, and you don't give quarter to your enemies; oh no!" And as Bertrand extended his hand (which appeared to him to be a veritable paw) to take the drawing, she withdrew it with a bewitching gesture, and hid it under her shawl with *such* an arch little nod of defiance.

"You talk of giving quarter to enemies, Miss M'Killop, just as if I counted you as one. Why?"

"Because it is true, Mr Cameron."

"True!"

"Yes; you don't like me. I always know when people don't like me by their eyes. I think a great many people don't like me, and I always want them to tell me why. Now, be frank; look me in the face and tell me why."

"Whe—whe—when I look you in the face, I swear——"

"Oh, please, don't swear; but, look! look! —oh, do look at that! What is it? A real orange butterfly! Oh, pray, catch it for me! —do, pray, Mr Cameron!"

Bertrand was up in an instant, performing all sorts of acrobatic feats with his legs and arms and hat, dodging the butterfly out and in the trees, and among the tangle of blackthorn and wild rose and honeysuckle, butting his head against projecting branches, tearing his clothes and wounding his body in many places. The butterfly entered into the spirit of the thing, and flew low, and Bertrand had a quick three minutes with it, resulting in its capture.

He brought it carefully under his cap: she bent forward over the cap; he bent forward over the cap. The streamers of a ribbon round her neck were lifted by a little breath of wind, and lay on his shoulder; her hand touched his; he trembled all over, so that he collapsed heavily on the cap, the cap on the butterfly, the butterfly into powder.

"Oh, Mr Cameron, how cruel! how cruel! You have killed the poor, dear, beautiful butterfly," and she looked at him reproachfully, with eyes that expressed tears if they shed none.

What sensibility! Still the ribbons lay on his shoulder (the accolade of a thousand knighthoods would have been valueless compared with that blessed contact), and, in her emotion, her hand still clasped the cap—would have touched his hand—but he shrank from *that*.

"Are you sorry?" she said, after a pause, during which Bertrand felt as if his eyes were being drawn out like telescopes by the attraction of hers—"are you sorry?"

"I am very sorry—very, very sorry." His voice shook, and changed its key with every second word.

"I believe you are very sorry," she said, slowly withdrawing her eyes, and moving back so that the ribbons glided from his shoulder, gently, lingeringly, inch by inch—" and I forgive you."

What magnanimity!

" To prove that I am not an enemy," said Bertrand, " I can show that at least I have tried to please you; I have executed your commission."

" What commission, Mr Cameron?"

" White heather. Look!"—and he withdrew, from the interior of his waistcoat, the hermit of the corrie, looking rather jaded, to be sure, from long contact with a flannel shirt that had been shot in, and fished in, and fainted in, all in a mean temperature of 90° Fahrenheit or so.

" Oh, how kind! how very good of you! to think of me, and when you were ill! Thank you; thank you so much."

" Let me dip it in the river to freshen it before you take it."

" Oh no, no! I will take it *just* as you brought it. I never thought you would trouble about it, or think of it any more."

Bertrand made a tremendous effort, and murmured, in rapid, husky jerks, " I never thought of anything else. I would never—have gone to the hill to-day—except to get it. I wish it was a thousand times prettier—I wish it was worthier of you."

"Can anything be worthier of a child of the mountains than the most beautiful thing that grows upon them?"

"Oh yes—everything is worthier—of you."

Puck was at him again. "But I am sorry you had the trouble and the fatigue," continued Eila; "I am afraid you made yourself ill in looking for it. How kind of you! but if you made yourself ill in looking for it, I shall never forgive myself. Tell me, did you?"

"Oh no, not at all; I would have been ill——" He was going to try to add, "a thousand times, and died a thousand times, in such a cause," or some absurdity of the sort, but Eila turned it off.

"Should you, at any rate? Then I am satisfied, and" (rather a tame climax) "really very much obliged."

"Will you do me a favour?" cried Bertrand.

"If I can I will—what is it?"

"Will you wear the heather this evening?"

"Oh yes; I will begin now. See!" and she placed it in the bosom of her dress. A————h!

"Please tell me a story, Mr Cameron," she resumed suddenly, after the flower was adjusted.

"A story, Miss M'Killop! but what sort of story?"

"About battles and adventures; I like reading about them, and it would be delightful to hear about them from a real soldier who has been in them, and done them, and been made a prisoner and wounded. You *have* been wounded, of course?"

"No—yes—very slightly—a mere nothing" (in allusion to a tremendous black eye from a brickbat at Killygobslithereen,—painful but not romantic, and certainly not the incident for the moment)—"a mere nothing; but no man likes to talk about his own exploits," particularly, he might have added, when he has to draw exclusively for them on his imagination—before dinner. "So if you really want to hear a little romance of war, I'll tell you about an adventure in the Indian Mutiny of one of our fellows—Gibbs."

"Gibbs! what an ugly name! rhymes to 'fibs,' doesn't it?"

Bertrand admitted that it did, and also to "ribs," for the matter of that; but Gibbs, notwithstanding his prosodial misfortunes, was really a tremendous fellow—a V.C. even. Still Eila would have none of Gibbs, though his deeds might have shed lustre on a De Montmorency. "Well, then, another of my friends really did a splendid thing at the Taku Forts, and had such an adventure in the Summer Palace afterwards; shall I tell you about that?"

"What was his name?"

The hero's name was really Barton, but Bertrand saw at once that while rhyming to "tartan" he was unfit for service, so he eliminated the disqualifying letter and said "Baron."

"Yes, I would like to hear about Mr Baron."

And Bertrand told her a terrible anecdote, all about junks and joss-houses and gingalls, and the yells of the Celestials, and the terrible British cheer, and mandarins, and the Brother of the Sun and Moon, and his silks and furs and jewels, and the palatial bonfire,— through all which the sword of the terrible

Barton meandered like a streak of lightning caught and drilled for the occasion to warlike purposes. The story was lengthy; it had outfalls of episode, and a pretty broad dreary current of its own, and, during its progress, Bertrand made a discovery—angels can yawn. The discovery depressed him; the full-flowing river of his speech rolled on with a more languid movement, and the lightning of Barton the destroyer, began to shed rather sickly gleams on its sluggish wave. Still it went on to a point where Barton, after having lost an arm from a round-shot, received a sword-thrust through the body and a contusion on the head, and become reluctantly insensible, might reasonably be supposed to have terminated his exploits; and here Eila, assuming the close of the narrative, thanked Bertrand for it, with great alacrity; said it was most interesting, and what a surprising person Mr Baron must be— and probably she might have found him so to be, if she had had patience, and got beyond the mere threshold of the anecdote; for, of course, she had only heard Act I.; and fellows like Barton, as a rule, never succumb; the lopping off of a limb or two only clears them, as it were, for more vigorous action; and if they ever condescend to die at all, it is in the picturesque Chevy-Chase attitude of fighting on their stumps.

Bertrand acquiesced in the dropping of the curtain; he felt that he was not shining; and indeed what kind of figure can a wax-taper cut, when flickering in the full beams of Hyperion?—and so he allowed Eila even to imagine Mr Barton's death. That, at least, lent him an interest which could not belong to one whose voice was even at that hour contributing to "the thunder of the captains and the shouting" in the Long Valley.

"If I had been a man, I *must* have been a soldier!" cried Eila, as a sort of funeral-shot over Barton and his glories.

It flashed across Bertrand's mind that he had better hum (archly), "If I was a lad, for a soldier I'd go," but he curbed the inclination as profane, and said instead, "Surely you would not have preferred to be a man?"

"Oh, indeed I should: do you think a woman's life *can* be a very happy one, except under very peculiar circumstances? How would you like to be *au convent* under the shadow of Craiginfrioch for the rest of your days, or some place just as bad?"

"That fate can never be yours, except by choice."

"It is generally a choice of evils in the world, is it not? for a woman, at least," said Eila, with a graceful little shrug.

"Oh, please, don't speak like that," cried Bertrand, with genuine earnestness. It gave him a quick pain to think of so bright and beautiful a being living in any atmosphere save one of perpetual joy, radiance, and delight. "I think women," he said, "beautiful women, clever women, and, above all, good women, even without being beautiful or clever, have as fine a career, if they choose to accept it, as any man can have."

"You are beginning to be grave—please, don't."

"I beg your pardon, I won't. But think of us poor men with compassion. If all the beautiful women in the world were withdrawn or transformed, what would become of us? What would the knight in the lists have been without the Queen of Beauty or his lady-love in the gallery?"

"That is very pretty! I like that. Are you fond of poetry?"

"Devoted to it."

"And music?"

"There I am a fanatic."

"Oh, I see now why Morna and you are such allies!"

"Allies?" The villain was on the point of denying an alliance too good for nine hundred and ninety-nine out of a thousand of his sex. Love, which conquers all things, walks lightly over loyalty, generosity, and all the verities. "Allies?" he repeated; and then, as a compromise, "*Are* we allies?"

"You act as if you were, at all events, don't you?" and then, with sudden eagerness, (who can say from what source?) "and you may be very proud to be an ally of hers, because there is no one the least like her. She is too good to be any one's ally. It makes one better to be with her: she is the only person in all the world I like."

How beautiful she looked, thus animated for her friend! And how delightful to know that she cared for no one else (" the present company," she had expressly stated, " is always excepted"); and what a goodly thing was a beautiful girl's love for another—girl! Slightly inconsistent though at times, as now appeared; for, instantly after her glowing eulogy, she laid her hand on Bertrand's arm, and said, " Hush! hush! look, here is Morna; lie down and hide." Whereupon the wretch " crouched fawning in the weed," and Morna passed away on the other side. She looked jaded and tired; she was carrying her own basket slung over her shoulder, and her rod. Her eyes were bent on the ground; she was not looking very happy. At sight of her, some emotion of—what was it? —pity? remorse? of conscious desertion and betrayal?—something unpleasant, at any rate, struck into Bertrand's heart, and with it an impulse to dash across the river and carry her things for her, and be "jolly" to her generally. But he looked up to his beautiful companion, who sat leaning against a tree twined with murderous honeysuckle; and as the tree was clasped in that deadly-sweet embrace, so did the influence of those enthralling eyes wind itself round his heart, and choke the generous emotion. Retributive justice halts not always; and in about a minute Eila said, "You had better follow her now." This was illogical, also unpleasant.

"Oh, please, don't send me away," said Bertrand.

"You came out to fish with her, you know; and so you belong to her—for the afternoon."

"But will you come too? You have no idea how interesting it is to watch Miss Grant fishing;—she catches lots of them—every minute—most exciting; do come."

"Thanks—no; I must go back to my novel: I can think of nothing else till it is finished. Please don't mind me. I shall find my way home by the bridge. If you ford the river here you will be able to overtake Morna. Poor dear Morna! looking so tired and bored all by herself! Do run away quickly, please."

"And you will wear *it?*" languishingly.

"*It?* What, Mr Cameron?"

"The heather!"

"Oh, the heather! Oh yes, if you wish it, and it isn't dead by the evening. Good-bye —*au revoir.*"

So, with an east wind whistling in every nook and cranny of his soul, Bertrand took the water and followed "poor dear Morna."

Memoranda — angels yawn — are sometimes illogical, and always incomprehensible. He did not long follow Morna in a straight course, but soon diverged to the left, and, circling round at top-speed, managed to head her, and was fishing at the point where he ought to have been when, half an hour later, she came up to pass him again. Few and short were the words they spoke. Morna had had bad sport; Bertrand none—as represented in his basket, that is; and eventually, after various passings and repassings, they walked home together much as they had walked out together, both regretting, with wonder and animation, the total and surprising failure of Campbell's new "spider."

Pigott came in late from the hill, and found Bertrand already— rather prematurely—dressed for dinner, and about to descend to the drawing-room.

"Well, Bertrand, all right again?"

"Oh, all right, thanks."

"Been out?"

"Just took a stroll by the river for a bit. How have you done to-day?"

"Pretty well; dogs rather demoralised,

though. Look here, I found that heather for Miss What's-her-name; rather a fine specimen, isn't it?"

"Beautiful, yes; but I found a bit on the hillside, and have given it to her; so we can keep yours for our own drawing-room table."

"No, I shall give this to her. I've had rather a time of it with the thing. I stuck it in my cap to keep fresh, and it kept tumbling out, and lost me a brace of grouse by getting across my eyes at the critical moment; besides, the only ptarmigan I saw to-day rose when I was digging it up; so I'll give it to her, and tell her about it as a hint not to go bothering again."

"As you please," said Bertrand, and went to the drawing-room.

No one there. Presently in came Mr M'Killop—bother *him!*—no *tête-à-tête* was now possible; then came Mrs M'Killop—bother *her!*—how loud she looked! then came Morna, bother—no, not exactly that—and immediately after entered Eila (in blue); but, alas! where was the white heather? Not there, at all events, where it would have looked so well, in harmony with a blue dress. It was an occasion to sulk a little, and Bertrand did so (in the window). The sulking was dramatic, *bien entendu*. There was nothing in his heart but humble grief and a sense of merited discomfiture.

Presently in walked Pigott, cool, trim, dry, in his hand the bunch of heather. He walked up to Eila, held out the offering with—

"This is the vegetable you wanted, Miss M'Killop, is it not?"

"Oh, Captain Pigott!" cries Eila. "Oh, so many thanks! how beautiful!"

She takes it;—it is no longer heather—it is amaranth—although the gift of Pigott.

"On the very tip-top of Craiginfrioch did you find it?"

"On the very tip-top—where there are ptarmigan!"

"On the very *tip-top*, where there are ptarmigan! Delightful!"

"The only ptarmigan I saw to-day rose when I was tearing up that plant."

"How tiresome! and did you carry it *all* the way down, yourself?"

"All the way in my hat; as a proof, it tumbled across my eyes, and made me miss a brace of grouse."

"What a pity! but how kind of you to get it for me, and to go missing grouse and ptarmigans to oblige me! Thank you so much—it is quite beautiful; a finer plant, I think, than Mr Cameron brought me, though it was very pretty too. Oh, by the by, Mr Cameron, I am so sorry I couldn't do what you wished; the poor thing was too much faded." Bertrand was understood to say that it didn't signify, and Eila went on, "But this comes instead, and I shall wear *it*. Shall I wear it, Captain Pigott?"

"Oh, by all means."

"Then I will," and she ran airily to the mirror and placed one bunch in her bosom and another in her hair (coquettishly)—and then turned round, putting her hands down by her side, with the fairy-like gesture of a playful child, for inspection. "How does it do? Is it pretty?"

Pretty! but Bertrand could say nothing, and Pigott remarked, jocularly, "Yes, it looks very well; it literally does honour to your head and heart."

He was getting just a little beyond human endurance—this—this *groundling*.

Pigott's seniority constituted him Mrs M'Killop's daily escort to the dining-room, and Eila fell to Bertrand. "Wasn't it kind of Captain Pigott to get this for me from the tip-top of Craiginfrioch, where the ptarmigans are?" she inquired confidentially of Bertrand, as they passed from the drawing-room; "but do you think, *entre nous*, it bored him? I should be in despair if I thought I had bored him."

"It was a great privilege for Captain Pigott to have the happiness of doing anything to give you pleasure," said Bertrand, grimly.

"He *is* very good-natured and kind, is he not?"

"Very."

"He has such a nice kind face, has he not?"

"Yes."

"Like a good dog's, isn't it?"

"Ha! ha! yes, not bad that—rather like a dog's, certainly."

"A good dog's though, and that is not the least laughable, for a good dog's face is the pleasantest face in the world—to me."

Not being a dog of any sort, there was clearly nothing for Bertrand but to sulk after that. All through dinner Eila was perversely enchanting, and Bertrand was in and out of the sulks a score of times at the least; the trying part of it all being that she never appeared to know when he was supposed to be in a state of dignity, and when in a state of delight, penitence, worship, or what not. The same sort of thing went on in the drawing-room, where Eila cajoled her father and the two ecartists into playing whist with her, so that Morna and Bertrand were left to a dismal *tête-à-tête*; then she threw up the cards after the first rubber, alleging a headache; then she coaxed Morna to sing, and when Bertrand approached, with earnest pleading eyes, to seat himself by her, snubbed him instantly by rising, and "though so sorry to be unsociable, really wishing to sit quite quiet by the window, for her headache's sake, if he didn't mind." And so the evening passed, and much in the same way passed the next few days, as regarded the relations of Eila and Morna and Bertrand; the latter now like the Peri at the gate of Paradise, disconsolate, now admitted for one instant within the glittering portals, and the next expelled from it by the lightning eye of the avenging angel. Like Jeanie pining for Jamie, he began to "gang like a ghaist and caredna to spin"—that is, to shoot or fish, or eat or drink, or sleep or hold commune with

Pigott or any other flesh of man, save only with her, who by a word could make him the blessedest of mortals, and by a look could cause him to peak and pine and dwindle. He had no quarrel with Pigott, quite the reverse —but he avoided a *tête-à-tête* with that officer as he would have shunned the plague, ignoring the smoking-room and the boudoir sacred to *bonne camaraderie*, and rushing to bed of nights, with a hasty "tired as a dog, old fellow—can*not* smoke to-night—really can't." Pigott, of course, knew the state of the case as well as, if not better than, his friend; but though he said to himself that the present juncture was not gay, still he was certain that to endure it was the less of two evils, the alternative being to become confidant, and listen to his friend's eternal maunderings about *that* girl, for ever harvesting with her unquiet eyes.

END OF THE FIRST VOLUME.

PRINTED BY WILLIAM BLACKWOOD AND SONS, EDINBURGH.

www.ingramcontent.com/pod-product-compliance
Lightning Source LLC
Chambersburg PA
CBHW030326240426
43673CB00040B/1283